Approaches to Religious Education

ISBN 034018437X

Approaches to Religious Education

Margaret Evening

UNIVERSITY OF LONDON PRESS LTD

ISBN 0 340 18437 X

First published 1972 by Hodder & Stoughton Ltd
First published as a Unibook 1974

University of London Press Ltd,
St Paul's House, Warwick Lane, London EC4P 4AH

Printed offset litho and bound in Great Britain by
Cox & Wyman Ltd, London, Fakenham and Reading

To Martin, my Godson

ACKNOWLEDGEMENTS

The author and publishers gratefully make acknowledgement to: the Chief Education Officer of the London Borough of Sutton Local Education Authority for permission to reproduce photographs and extracts of the work of the girls of Wallington High School; the Chief Education Officer, West Riding Local Education Authority for permission to reproduce page 52 of the West Riding syllabus; Howard M. King Ltd., Croydon, for photographs of dance drama; David Draper of Gipsy Hill College for photographs of models; and Sue Rattenbury of Gipsy Hill College for photographs of stained glass windows.

ACKNOWLEDGMENTS

[illegible]

CONTENTS

ILLUSTRATIONS

between pages 96 *and* 97

PREFACE

So much is now being written about the ways in which Religious Education may be taught, in an attempt to 'redeem the misspent time that's past', that perhaps we are in danger of swamping ourselves and our staff rooms with an excess of material on new 'ways in'. We can spend so much time reading *how* it should be done, that we are almost afraid to get on with it. And, of course, there is the other danger of becoming so self-conscious, Goldman-conscious, Piaget-conscious and syllabus-conscious—that we never 'do what comes naturally', which is often the most enduring way of educating children religiously. Some of the best Religious Education (particularly at the secondary school level) is the result of a pupil/teacher relationship which leads to perfectly natural conversation and spontaneous discussion. If something has come alive for us, it will communicate itself readily to those we teach, and it would surely be regrettable if this were stultified by an over-concern to analyse the kind of concepts we are inculcating (necessary though it certainly is to make some careful analyses).

However, spurred on by the recognition that with increasing years of experience I find R.E. teaching becoming more difficult rather than less so, I dare to produce this book in the hope that it will encourage those about to embark on this exciting branch of teaching; and, having taught a wide variety of subjects, I find it still remains *the* most exciting subject in the curriculum. For all the difficulties, I should hate not to be in the front line!

This is not a handbook, or a discussion of the philosophies behind Religious Education. It is intended to be a very simple, practical aid to newcomers to the subject, to stimulate ideas and suggest practical ways for their implementation. It may serve to remind us that the 'front' on which R.E. advances is a very broad one. To use an analogy, R.E. is not so much a geyser as a series of hot springs, not one vast spout but bubblings up all over the place, numerous explosive eruptions which cannot be confined to one small area but are surprisingly widespread, so widespread that it would be impossible to make a fully comprehensive survey within the scope of one book. The reader will inevitably find some aspects of R.E. that have not been dealt with here though an attempt has been made to show how R.E. 'erupts' through community service, team teaching, group projects, counselling as well as 'straight' Bible study.

Teachers accustomed to more formal methods may well express concern that, by following some of these ideas, it would seem that children will receive far less Bible teaching than previously. It may well be that they will cover less actual biblical material but we hope that what they do learn will be extremely relevant to them because every effort has been made to relate it to their own experience and their learning in other disciplines. I should be sorry if this book gave the impression that the Bible plays only a small part in R.E. these days. In fact I have tried to show how the many varied approaches may be thoroughly Bible orientated. My intention is to emphasise that more and more we must examine the skills which are needed to introduce the Bible to children of all ages without evoking a hostile response.

The teacher, who believes that God is 'above all and in all and through all', has often, with the authority of the Agreed Syllabus and the co-operation of colleagues, a real opportunity of 'proclaiming' this all-pervading God and of doing his, albeit insignificant, bit to break down the mythical barriers between the sacred and secular. Every subject in the curriculum can yield *in its own terms* some facet of religious understanding. We do not merely 'use' these subjects to convey something about the Almighty. Rather we seek to find God in them. With this kind of approach, we should begin to see a shift from the idea of a God 'up there' to a God who really is 'the ground of our being' and the meaning and purpose of all existence.

The contents of this book are designed primarily, but not

exclusively, for the encouragement and help of secondary school teachers of Religious Education. I hope, however, that some of it will prove useful to those engaged in primary school teaching. Some, at least, of the ideas will be easily adapted to different age-groups.

I gladly express my thanks to all those who have made this book possible and acknowledge the real debt I owe to many who have helped me in my years as an R.E. specialist. In particular I should like to thank Miss A. M. Mark, M.A., the Headmistress of Wallington High School for Girls, Surrey, who gave me great liberty to experiment in this field and who encouraged me so much even in the less orthodox enterprises; my colleagues in the R.E. department at Wallington, who were valiant in their support; and not least of all, the girls themselves who made it all so enjoyable and worthwhile by their responsiveness and interest.

My deepest appreciation and thanks must go too to the Rev. W. H. Davies, B.A., B.D., for his reading of the proofs and kindly comments and criticisms, to his wife, Mrs. J. M. Davies, for the arduous task (so readily undertaken) of typing the scripts, and to Peter Cousins, M.A., B.D., Principal Lecturer in Divinity at Gipsy Hill College of Education for much valuable advice and encouragement.

1
LIFE THEMES

When people discover that you teach R.E., they often start reminiscing about their own schooldays and recollect the kind of things they did in Scripture. Sometimes one shudders at the revelations and earnestly hopes that the passing years have caused the memory to play tricks and touch things up a little. Yet we do know that, in days gone by, the Scripture lesson sometimes consisted of learning chunks of the Bible by heart or even the catechism.

The story is told of one young teacher who drilled his class daily (one could almost say religiously) in the catechism. Each day he began with the same child, asking round the class in turn the same question and getting the same prompt reply. Then one day an Inspector called and decided to test the class on the catechism. Picking on one child at random, he asked, 'Who made you?' The child was silent. The Inspector tried another child with the same negative response, then another and another. Eventually, in exasperation he said, 'Well, surely *someone* knows who made them?' A timid little girl in the front raised her hand and said, 'Please sir, the boy whom God made has gone to the lavatory!'

One friend, recalling the excellent scriptural teaching she had received, claimed, 'I can still recite the names of all the Kings of Israel'. Inwardly, I wondered what kind of religious insights this knowledge (laudable as it may be) had given. Did it deepen her understanding of the nature of man, and the problems of his relationship to people and to God? Did it give any helpful solutions to ethical problems?

I recollect that in my final year in the junior school, we recited the judgement scene from Matthew 25 regularly every week (following straight on from our tables) with the result that I can still repeat that passage and the other favourite, Revelation 21. I don't remember if the first conjured up scenes of celestial sheep trials, but I know that the second left me with a vivid image of a complete city of gold emerging from the clouds like literal castles in the air. I thought the language was beautiful but I had no idea what it meant.

Testing the biblical knowledge of quite young African children revealed an astonishingly accurate memorisation of many of the genealogies. It was impossible to fault them on the orders of begetting, and they were most reliable authorities when it came to sorting out intricate and involved relationships. With their strong emphasis on tribal descent and relationship, this had great appeal for them, but we sometimes despaired of ever leading them away from the rut of purely factual knowledge (considerable as it was) to the far more important inner understanding of the biblical message.

R.E. lessons in the past have often consisted simply of the reading of a Bible story which acquainted children with the names of heroes and the nature of their deeds—but that was all. In the pupils' minds it probably ranked on a par with the adventures of Ulysses, or it may have been that the stories of shipwrecks, giants, and the binding of strong men were strongly reminiscent of Gulliver's travels.

Methods have changed now—and thank God for that! Almost all the new syllabuses suggest a thematic approach to Religious Education. The general approach of the older ones was to start from the Bible and try to cover the major part of it during the school career (cf. Newsom Report, *Half our Future* (H.M.S.O.), p. 57).

Whilst one would still hope that by the time a pupil *leaves* school he has a working knowledge of the contents of the Bible, it will not be arrived at by a systematic study from Genesis to Revelation. It is far more important that he should have grasped certain biblical insights and concepts than have an all-inclusive grasp of the major events of Jewish history from 1,000 B.C. to A.D. 70. In any case, it would seem extremely unwise to attempt an introduction to *all* the biblical material available. A careful selection of material suited to the particular age-group being taught is essential if the pupil is not to develop a deep dislike of the Bible and of its truths. Dr. Goldman has exposed clearly and disturbingly some of the damage done to children's conceptual thinking by an insufficiently selective choice of biblical material in the teaching of R.E.

Failures in R.E. are often due to the fact that the children are bored and cannot see that the subject has any relevance for their own present-day situation. It is in an attempt to combat this condition that life themes were first introduced and are advocated as the right approach. Certainly to adopt such a teaching method is not simply to follow the precepts of Dr. Goldman but of our Lord himself, who in his parables always started from the real life situation and led on to deeper truths. The important thing to note is that, in the teaching of Jesus, there were always depths, behind the seemingly simple story, which people would discover at varying levels. He recognised that some would grasp the mysteries of the Kingdom and others would miss them altogether. The same is true today. On the surface, it may seem, in using this technique in the classroom, that pupils are just having a great time collecting photos of the family, or learning how bread comes to our tables, studying the pop scene, or making models, hearing about the divorce laws or the Industrial Relations Bill, with the result that they may be a little less bored but absolutely no nearer spiritual truths. This could be true, of course, and especially for the teacher who is uncertain of his own position *vis-à-vis* the Bible and his own faith; it is decidedly easier to start from the present-day situation than from the Bible—and he may well get stuck there. But let not the onlookers to the R.E. scene be too hasty to judge the end by the beginning. Jesus could have been accused of wasting people's time by telling them stories about agricultural disappointments, robberies with violence, silly sheep, giant mustard trees, and jerry-built houses.

Thematic teaching is child-related

Through his extensive research into *Religious Thinking from Childhood to Adolescence*, Dr. Goldman claims that 'we have too long had Religious Education that is "Bible-centred" and now we need to work out one which is "child-centred"'. Dr F. H. Hilliard objects to the term, however, since child-centred learning implies that religion is derived solely from within. It is 'man's response to the given', and therefore Dr. Hilliard prefers the term 'child-related'.*

The thematic approach makes possible child-related teaching—in that themes may be introduced to suit the needs of various age-groups drawing in the experience of the children as well as the discreet and advised choice of biblical material and relating the two. So, starting from the known, the child may be led on to the unknown and into increasingly meaningful concepts of God.

It is across-subject related

Not only is the teaching related to the child's experience, but it is also related to other subjects, so that education is seen as a whole and Religious Education as a valid, self-authenticating part of that whole. 'One of the ways of giving reality to Religious Education is by across-subject teaching, exploring a theme in several different ways.' (*West Riding Syllabus*, p. 2.)

In the infant school the subject divisions are blurred anyway, and to some extent this is true of the junior school. There are still many secondary schools, however, where (subject divisions being necessarily observed) R.E. is regarded as a rather lesser brother, requiring fewer qualifications, lower academic standards, and holding (ironically) little value for the life beyond (i.e. in terms of future careers, prospects of good jobs and financial success). Thematic teaching helps to demonstrate the interdependence and parity of different academic disciplines, and is certainly valuable in sixth form integrated studies.

* Dr. F. H. Hilliard, *The Teacher and Religion* (Clarke).

It encourages study in greater depth

To take a theme and explore it in depth is to provide a unity in learning. Besides acquiring knowledge on the horizontal plane, it leads to discovery in the round. It may not cover as extensive an area, but what is discovered will be more lasting and meaningful than the wider but more superficial knowledge. Such a method has all the satisfaction of taking a deep draught rather than a series of frustrating little sips. For example, the Temple features in many of the biblical accounts, and knowledge of its history may be acquired in a very fragmentary way. How much more interesting to take an imaginary journey to Jerusalem and the Temple area (through slides or films), look at the contemporary situation, and then let the Temple tell its own story and the major events in its life—collating material from Old and New Testaments and contemporary historians such as Josephus. Through such a topic the student would surely gain insights into Hebrew concepts of God, and the solidarity of the people of God, the massive significance of sacrifice and the penitential system, and the awe-ful sense of the holiness of God. An attempt at such a theme is included in this chapter. Probably a suitable study for sixth and fifth formers, it could be reduced in quantity to suit younger age-groups. It is the sort of technique a historian might use in preparing a class for a visit to the Tower of London or Hampton Court.

To stand on Westminster Bridge and gaze at the Thames is to gaze at 'liquid history'. What stories that river could tell, had it a voice! Similarly what a fascinating study could be made of the historical events surrounding the Jordan river.

It encourages willing Bible study

It is often difficult to encourage the actual reading of the Bible in secondary schools, even though many authorities give presentation copies to every pupil in the third or fourth year. (Sometimes the

Gideons present New Testaments to all first-year pupils in the secondary school.) In thematic studies, however, the Bible is at least used as one of a number of source books, and in their search for information pupils will freely turn to recommended passages without prejudice, scorn or embarrassment. By this method classes may be encouraged to use their Bibles far more than if they were simply reading up a story to cement in their memories something that had already been told them. Any R.E. teacher will know the awful groans that can go up when pupils are told to 'Get out your Bibles and turn to page . . . .' When they are encouraged to start from a discussion and examination of their own contemporary situation (e.g. economic and social injustice) and then search for parallel situations in the Bible, it not only enables them to see that the human dilemma has not changed unduly in the last three or four thousand years, that man is still greedy, grasping, rebellious and deceitful, but also the discovery helps to awaken a new kind of respect for the Scriptures.

For example, in a study on the theme of health in different climates, tropical and sub-tropical as well as temperate, talks from missionary doctors on leprosy, yaws, the many causes of blindness and cataracts and other endemic diseases, led to a most willing search for biblical confirmation of such conditions in the Holy Land. A study of some of the health laws in Leviticus and prohibitions of various foods enjoined upon the Hebrews in their nomadic wanderings, were seen to be not just a string of petty rules but eminently sensible. It gave new meaning to some of the New Testament healing miracles. The class came to realise how the 'Bartimaeuses', with their begging bowls, were and are a most common sight, how daring it was of Jesus actually to touch a leper, and how extraordinarily tough he must have been physically to have lived the sort of life he did in constant contact with sick and diseased people, and yet, apparently, not to succumb to illness himself.

This was followed up by some study of the activities of the World Health Organisation, and what is being done today through various agencies to help underdeveloped countries fight such diseases as leprosy, yaws, malnutrition and its inevitable consequences.

They were told of some of the very successful measures taken against malaria and sleeping sickness and of the men whose persistent researches led to the discovery of life-saving drugs.

The theme finally dealt with the importance in the thinking and attitude of Jesus to physical health and wholeness, and wherein lay his priorities (using as examples the healing of the paralytic borne of four, the woman with a haemorrhage, the teaching on spiritual surgery in Matthew 5, the healing of the Gadarene demoniac, references to those occasions when he declined to heal).

Some of the most exciting studies being undertaken at the moment are those in biblical archaeology, and this suggests to us a further possibility of thematic learning. A theme which explored the findings of archaeological research might have a limited appeal, perhaps to a small group rather than an entire class (but in sixth form work it is possible to offer a choice of themes and pursue them concurrently with different groups). However, to make a study of works such as Keller's *The Bible as History*, or Thompson Davies's *Biblical Archaeology* or Sir Leonard Woolley's *Digging up the Past* and *Bible and Spade*, or G. E. Wright's *An Introduction to Biblical Archaeology*, can be a most profitable and stimulating exercise. Inevitably the field would need to be narrowed down. But, even taking a very small area of study such as a character study of Solomon, reading up all the information made available to us through archaeology of the exploits of this amazing business tycoon, would provide not simply a fascinating study, but in many cases corroborative evidence of the biblical accounts (which might in the past have been doubted or unnoticed). Certainly, it would enlarge the group's understanding and appreciation of this king enormously. Similar studies could be carried out taking Jerusalem as the focal point (N.B. the way in which, almost by chance, the water course used by David to storm and capture the city, was discovered), or Ur of the Chaldees, or the ancient cities that feature in the Canaanite conquest, etc.

Cautions to be noted in this method of teaching

It will be seen that most of the above suggestions are suitable for more senior classes, but one or two themes primarily intended for junior classes have been developed and included at the end of this chapter. These could be related to almost any age-group in the junior school, but certain cautions must be noted.

IT IS VERY TAXING WORK FOR THE TEACHER

This kind of teaching does require of the teacher far more imagination, ingenuity, flexibility and preparation than the telling of a Bible story followed by the illustrating of it, or the making of a model. The teacher needs to have not only a fair number of ideas himself, but the ability to arouse interest and stimulate ideas in the children. If the teacher is not prepared for the sheer hard work involved in this method, stirring up the imagination of the class, planning, organising and carrying through effectively practical follow-up projects, keeping the goals and the object of the exercise always in sight so that, without cramping the children's style or damping their enthusiasm, the class is kept on a steady course that will leave them with lasting impressions and insights, it is far better not attempted. But if he really wants to make this part of education come alive, and is prepared for the cost, it is a most effective technique.

THERE MUST BE SUCH INTEGRATION THAT IT IS TRULY RELIGIOUS EDUCATION

It is so easy, however, to choose a theme and allow it to meander over so broad a field that it embraces every possible kind of information, however tenuous the relationship, which results in a scrapbook on the subject, rather than a body of knowledge in depth. And in the scrapbook approach it is all too easy to think that if amongst all the accumulation of information, a couple of Bible stories are dragged in, this justifies it as *Religious Education.* Thematic teaching in R.E. is *not* a fascinating discussion of everything under the sun with a bit of God-talk thrown in. As has been hinted earlier, specifically biblical and doctrinal aspects of the theme must be truly integrated, and the desired goal clearly kept in view. For example, in the theme on homes, included here, the material ranges over a fairly wide area, but the thematic study will have failed utterly if, in the end, the children have a fair idea about igloos and long houses, but precious little understanding of the true meaning of home, and the central and most important factor in home life, an appreciation of all that goes into home-making and a desire to contribute to the mutual joy of the family. One would hope that it would lead to a sense of very real thankfulness for love of parents, brothers, sisters and pets which may even express itself in prayer, and imaginative, loving acts.

Similarly in the theme on journeys, there is a great deal of geographical material and many stories of explorations that inspire a sense of courage and adventure. Much useful general knowledge might be gained but unless these, together with stories of biblical journeys of faith and pilgrimage, lead on to some understanding of the progression in life (both of the individual and of the world community) with not only a beginning but a purposeful destiny, then this cannot be called Religious Education. Not all teachers would agree that:

> We are travelling home to God
> In the way our fathers trod.

nor would all subscribe to Wordsworth's view that:

> . . . as trailing clouds of glory do we come
> from God who is our home.

but there is a desperate hunger on the part of young people today to be assured that there is some purpose in life, and that it is leading somewhere. Following a theme on journeys at even a top junior school age can begin to plant the seed of this conviction, that will, we hope, gradually grow to fruition.

THE NEED FOR OPENNESS

One problem in all this is, that having clear goals, and making certain that there is real direction in the thematic study, the teacher needs always to be aware of the possibility that there may be more 'light and truth to break forth' than he had anticipated in his preparation. This is why there needs to be considerable flexibility *and* humble receptivity on the part of the teacher. As H. F. Mathews has pointed out (*Revolution in R.E.*, p. 136) the teacher needs to produce 'a syllabus which becomes an analysis of the sort of religious truth which can be assimilated by a child at any given age, and suggest representative experiences through which that truth can be evoked', at the same time recognising that he may not always gauge the extent and depth of the child's longing for and grasp of that truth.

THE NEED FOR CLEAR DIRECTION

A further reminder is perhaps apposite at this point. Whilst great freedom must be allowed as children explore a theme, there is also the need for very clear guidance. If they are asked to find out certain facts and pieces of information, then they must be told or shown where to find the relevant facts. If the school library does not meet the need of particular researches, then books should be borrowed from public libraries and kept for reference within the classroom for a specified period. It is not enough simply to tell a class to find out what it can about something without indicating sources of information. There is a need for a delicate balance between encouraging initiative and originality in the children and providing strong leadership and direction as the teacher.

Themes in the infant school

There is virtually no material in the suggested examples of life themes and biblical themes that would be of much help to infant school teachers. Thematic teaching has its place amongst the younger age ranges, but in a far more fluid way than in the junior, middle and secondary schools. One of the best accounts of the way in which themes with young children develop from situations as they occur is to be found in *A Diary for Teachers of Infants* by Freda and Philip Cliff (Hart-Davis). For example, they describe how freedom of movement in P.E. lessons and the pleasure of agility gave rise to a real and spontaneous sense of thankfulness for limbs and health. The birth of a baby brother linked up naturally with the story of the Nativity, and a general interest in family relationships.

Such a natural evolution of interest is surely the most effective way of giving children a religious interpretation of life, and in a sense the children provide their own syllabus. The teacher's task is to be aware of the opportunities as they arise and grasp and 'develop them to the point where their real religious significance is revealed' (*Learning for Life*, p. 30).

As the *West Riding Syllabus* puts it (p. 9): '. . . what matters most at this stage is not the use of religious words but the attitude of the teachers and the quality of the relationships in the classroom . . . Religious Education at this stage may be described in terms of thought, word and deed. Spiritual development is enriched by communicating ideas through paint, clay, music, language and other activities such as home-making in the Wendy house, caring for pets and helping other people. These activities are important in themselves but they may also be the starting point for children's own prayers of thankfulness and joy.'

Amongst the very youngest children, there should not be *undue* emphasis on relating everything to a theme. Very young children do not always see the relation between situations, and a forced relatedness in teaching would be meaningless and possibly downright unhelpful. There is something to be said for telling a story (including Bible stories) that has no particular bearing upon the theme being followed in other areas of study. It is not only that very young children do not always see the relationships as older children do, but their powers of sustaining interest in any one topic are far more limited. They do not need necessarily to explore the ideas of home in absolutely every area of their work—their story, poetry, painting, dance, geography, history, craft and R.E. If Religious Education at this age is to be really meaningful then the child must not be overwhelmed or overtaxed and certainly never bored. A syllabus cannot really do more than give a starting point. It is up to the teacher to be acutely sensitive to the right moments and the many opportunities for enlarging the child's experience, understanding and appreciation of life in its fullest sense.

Suggested life themes

[In each case the teacher will need to be selective. There is more material in these suggested themes than could be covered in the limited time available to R.E. on most time tables.]

HOMES

1. *'Our home'*

Start from the children's own homes with descriptions, ground-plans, discussion, etc. What do we enjoy most in our homes?

2. *A look at some of the castles and country houses of England*

Displays of photographs and guide books, and/or transparencies.

Possible school visit to an historic building, palace, house, etc.

Discussion on problem of living in rich large houses—upkeep, heating, lack of cosiness, sense of isolation.

3. *Homes of different countries*

Showing wide variety in architecture, style, etc.

Reasons for the difference because of climate (igloos, mud huts, log cabins).

Comparison of styles, e.g. the difference between modern Brazilian flats, a Papuan long house, an Austrian chalet, and a Bedouin tent.

4. *Palestinian homes in time of Jesus*

Models could be made from large cardboard boxes, showing both outer staircase to roof and interior with raised platform for family living. Various household items could also be made.

Use filmstrips or slides showing Palestinian villages. Let this information illuminate the stories of Jesus, e.g. A friend calling at midnight for bread which would involve disturbance of animals plus family. Thieves breaking through and stealing (because it was so easy in mudwalled houses). The Lost Coin. Lighting a house: lamp put on candlestick and not under bushel. Other biblical references: Peter on rooftop at Joppa. Elisha in the 'prophet's chamber', an extra little room sometimes built on roof.

5. *The home at Bethany*

Refer back to Jesus's early life in a normal Palestinian home probably attached to a carpenter's shop, up to the age of thirty. Once he started his ministry it meant no further homelife. He had no permanent dwelling place but, with his disciples, was dependent on hospitality wherever he went. Often he had to sleep rough. Cf. the young man from a comfortable home who asked to become a disciple. Jesus said, 'Foxes have holes and birds of the air have nests but the Son of Man has nowhere to lay his head'. Jesus loved to go to the home at Bethany where he could relax with Martha, Mary and Lazarus. The need for peace and quiet was strongest and Martha's insistence on good, nourishing meals was sometimes more disturbing than helpful. The reason why Jesus loved this home was not simply because of the creature comforts but because he could be utterly himself—no crowds, no demands made on him, no need to be on guard against those trying to 'catch him out'.

6. *Homes should be places where we can be entirely ourselves*

Discussion as to what this means. Does it mean that we have the right to be rude, intolerant and inconsiderate to those at home? It *does* mean that we do not have to try to impress or put on special 'best' behaviour, etc. It should be relaxing and comfortable to be with those who know us so very well and yet love us deeply.

7. *God is our home*

Why is this sometimes said? Discuss what seems to be our in-built homing device towards God: e.g. Augustine: 'Thou hast made us for Thyself and our hearts are restless till they find their rest in Thee.'

Children may quote from epitaphs they have seen on graves which speak of Heaven being our home. Heaven is where God is, and God knows us through and through yet loves us still. So, we do not need to put on any pretence before God. We can be entirely ourselves and therefore relax in this loving acceptance. And that very acceptance will make us want to please God more and more, just as love will prompt children to strive after achievements that will make their parents pleased and proud of them.

A note of warning

A teacher needs to know his class well before tackling this theme. If the school is in an area where children come from very widely differing backgrounds, or where 'home' consists of one or two rooms, then Section 1 will need to be greatly modified. What needs to be stressed throughout is not the size of the house and garden, and the luxuries in furniture and fitments, but the sense of being 'at home' with the people we love.

Section 6 needs very careful handling with the stress being placed upon the ideal, and the kind of homes we should all like to plan for the future, rather than working on the assumption that home as the children know it now is always a place where one can relax. It can be helpful and important to children from unhappy homes to discuss in a general way their ideas of an ideal home in a context in which the problem is distanced from *them*. At the same time for some it may provide the necessary outlets for more specific discussion. The teacher needs to be constantly aware that this may be a very sensitive area, and must tread most gently and lovingly.

JOURNEYS

(For ten to twelve year olds.)

Discuss and illustrate:

Ordinary, everyday journeys

To and from school by bus, car, train, on foot. The service to society of public transport; problems of delays, traffic jams, electricity cuts.

Special journeys
For holidays, e.g. coach, train, boat. Journeys abroad and, if you have children who have travelled (especially immigrant children) from abroad, let them discuss travel on sea (with transparencies), by air—photos of aerial views. (Illustrate with travel brochures and travel magazines.)

Methods of travelling abroad, e.g. horseback (link with pony trekking), by camel or elephant, metro or underground, caravan, e.g. R. L. Stevenson's *The Pedlarman.*

3. *Journeys into the unknown*
Journeys demanding courage and a sense of adventure, e.g. David Livingstone, opening up Africa. Gladys Aylward, setting out for an unknown destination. Arctic explorers such as Captain Scott. Space exploration. Abraham.

Journeys through some special need, e.g. Movements of nomadic tribes. Journeying of gypsies. Moving to a new district and moving house. (Stress the problems involved and the need for help and sympathy with those moving into our district.)

4. *'Incredible' journeys*
Possible examples: Migration of birds (help given by 'airways' to transport birds unable to fly). The incredible journey of the retriever, the bulldog and the Siamese cat. The von Trapp family's escape from Austria. Gladys Aylward leading the children away from danger. Henry Hudson's *Last Voyage*:

> 'Tomorrow, who can tell, the lucky chance awaits the fearless heart.
> The world is round and God is everywhere.
> And whilst our shalop floats we still can steer
> So, point her up, John King, Nor'west by north.
> We'll keep the valour of a steady course
> Amid the perils of uncertain ways
> And sail ahead, and leave the rest to God.'

5. *Journeys of special interest*
School visits.

A first visit to London: the excitement of seeing the capital and great buildings for the first time.

Jesus's first visit to Jerusalem at the age of twelve—excitement at seeing the Temple for the first time. Give descriptions of the magnificence of the Temple, possibly with a model.

Pilgrimages: Pilgrimage songs to accompany the carrying of the Ark into Jerusalem. Psalm 24. Psalm 91. The return of the exiles to Jerusalem. Isaiah 40. Stories of pilgrimages to famous shrines: The Pilgrims' Way to Canterbury illustrated from Chaucer. To Our Lady of Walsingham. To St. David's (cf. Elizabeth Goudge's description of a pilgrimage to St. David's in *The Child from the Sea*). *The Small Miracle* by Paul Gallico, (Pepino's journey to the Vatican to request permission to take Violetta, his donkey, to the local shrine of St. Peter).

6. *Life as a journey*
Introduce some carefully selected stories from *Pilgrim's Progress* by John Bunyan.

Life is an ongoing, onward moving thing like a journey (with a beginning and an end).

Cite examples of those who make great discoveries, and produce works of great creativity. It is a series of discoveries and achievements.

Introduce poems and narrative showing how people have thought of life as a journey, e.g. 'I said to the man who stood at the gate of the year' (*God Knows* by M. L. Haskins). 'To every man there openeth a way, and ways, and a way' (John Oxenham).

Recommended for choral speech:

Let me live in my house by the side of the road,
Where the race of men go by.
They are good, they are bad, they are weak, they are strong,
Wise, foolish—so am I!
Then why should I sit in the scorner's seat

Or hurl the cynic's ban?
Let me live in my house by the side of the road
And be a friend to man. (S. W. Foss.)
Cf. also 'The English Road' by G. K. Chesterton.

Theme on Worship

[For fifth and sixth form general studies.]

Introduction
What is worship? Work out several definitions, and collect the definitions of theologians and church leaders, e.g. William Temple: 'To worship is to quicken the conscience by the holiness of God, to feed the mind with the truth of God, to purge the imagination by the beauty of God, to open the heart to the love of God, to devote the will to the purpose of God. All this is gathered up in that emotion which most cleanses us from selfishness because it is the most selfless of all emotions—adoration.'

1. *The philosophical basis and cultural climate*
Discuss belief in God as a philosophical activity. Why believe in God or gods at all? Why do some people argue that God is something man dreams up to fulfil a psychological need? Others claim that God is made in the image of man: is this just cynicism?

(Study the arguments as presented in *Creeds and Controversies* by Miller and Pound (E.U.P.), who present the arguments from history, science, psychology, etc.) Note the universality of religious beliefs in all ages and in all countries.

Compare the various aspects involved in worship: the intellectual; the emotional; the volitional; the cultural; the aesthetic.

Make a study of various religions and see how these aspects vary in degree, e.g. compare philosophical Hinduism or Zen Buddhism to tribal religions in Thailand or Peru involving many superstitions and taboos. How much does environment and national temperament shape the religion of a country?

2. *Theological problems*
How we worship is often a matter of temperament and there will

always be the need for diversity in our forms of worship, but the divided church as we know it presents us with many theological problems.

Why did the church divide at the Great Schism and how has it gone on fragmenting? What issues were involved? Study some church history showing the major differences, e.g. the priestly versus prophetic emphasis. Note something of the Protestant emphasis on 'Justification by Faith' (with its stress on preaching of the Word of God leading to personal response in commitment and rebirth), and compare it with the Catholic emphasis on 'All is of Grace' which stresses the givenness of Christ and his gifts particularly through the Sacraments.

Compare the differences in forms of baptism, communion, ordination, reception into church membership or confirmation. (Note too other sacraments such as marriage, penance, holy orders, extreme unction, etc.)

Make a study of the heresies that have always plagued the Church down through the ages, and of their modern counterparts in the form of Jehovah's Witnesses, Scientology, Mormonism, etc. Note some of the movements of unity within the church through the Ecumenical movement. Trace the history of the World Council of Churches and various union schemes, e.g. the Church of South India, the Anglican/Methodist Union scheme. Find out if there are any ways in which local churches are uniting in worship or action or in sharing of buildings. What other positive steps forward in unity have been taken in the last decade?

3. *Art*

Observe the place that religious art has held in the history of art as a whole. Study some of the works of the great masters, i.e. their paintings, sculptures, engravings and architecture.

Look at examples of art from Africa, Malaysia, India, South America, etc., and note especially the carving of idols and other sacred objects.

Why do religious themes seem to appeal to artists and inspire their greatest works (N.B. the Old Testament view that the Spirit of God inspired all works of art and craftmanship e.g. Exodus 31:

3–5). Consider the attempts by modern artists to express the faith, and the use of modern art as an aid to worship, e.g. from *West Riding Syllabus*, p. 51:

Sutherland, Christ in Glory (Coventry Cathedral); Epstein, St. Michael and the Devil (Coventry Cathedral); Hutton, The glass screen with figures of the patriarchs, prophets, apostles and martyrs (Coventry Cathedral); Piper and Reyntiens, The baptistry window (Coventry Cathedral); Epstein, Majestas (Llandaff Cathedral); Epstein, Lazarus (New College, Oxford); Moore, Madonna and Child (St. Matthew's, Northampton); Bratby, Golgotha (St. Martin's College, Lancaster).

Study some modern art and discuss what it is saying to us. (Cf.: *Modern Art and the Death of a Culture* by Professor R. K. Rookmaaker.)

How has theology influenced the architecture of church buildings? e.g. the stress at present on congregational participation giving rise to central altars and round churches, the design of church premises being suited to community needs and not just church meetings.

Compare and contrast such buildings as: Chartres Cathedral and Liverpool Catholic Cathedral (N.B. film *Crown of Glass*), Coventry Cathedral and Guildford Cathedral. Other local examples of ancient and modern architecture.

Is it a fair generalisation to say that the Protestant emphasis on preaching accounts for central pulpits, and the Catholic emphasis on sacraments leads to central altars? Note the changes in new buildings, e.g. greater simplicity (even austerity) especially in continental Catholic churches; light, open and spacious buildings instead of the reduced lighting of stained-glass windows, plain stone tables rather than ornately carved altars, slim, needle-like spires rather than heavy towers and spires that require continual and costly upkeep.

Study the symbolism used in worship and its meaning.

Design a Baptist church giving theological reasons for the design, e.g. the doctrine of the gathered church, the one-ness round the Lord's Table, the centrality of preaching, the importance of believers' baptism—therefore a central baptistry.

Design a Quaker Meeting House bearing in mind especially the need for simplicity, and the gathered community. What, if any, focal point is there in such a meeting place? Design a parish church for a new housing estate remembering that the community may largely consist of young married couples, and may have to serve a multi-purpose function.

4. *Literature*

How are religious beliefs reflected in poetry, drama and the novel? Study examples, e.g.:

T. S. Eliot, *The Cocktail Party*, *The Family Reunion*, etc.; Christopher Fry, *Boy with a Cart*, *Sleep of Prisoners*; Jean Anouilh, *The Lark*; William Golding, *The Spire*; Graham Greene, *End of the Affair*; George Target, *Shop Stewards*.

How may literature best be incorporated in church worship? Discuss the relative literary beauty of the A.V., R.S.V., N.E.B. and *The Living Bible* versions of scripture. Discuss the place of drama in worship, and whether or not it makes a valuable impact:

(a) in celebrating special festivals
(b) in getting across biblical and ethical teaching
(c) in stirring up the conscience to social needs and injustices.

Cf. also Chapter 4, and its discussion of Drama. Suggest suitable examples and attend current local productions of religious drama.

5. *Liturgy*

Study as many different forms of Christian worship as possible and list their different appeals and values. What essentials are needed in an act of worship? e.g. varying kinds of leadership; congregational response and participation; meaningful yet beautiful language; biblical affirmations in the read and/or preached word; prayers including silences, acts of adoration and praise, confession and firm assurance of forgiveness (absolution), thanksgiving, intercession; offertory of money, bread and wine (in a service of holy communion), special gifts of toys, harvest produce, etc., at festivals; some overt reminder of the centrality of Christ (crucified, risen, ascended and reigning) in all worship, e.g. by carrying in of the cross by the Crucifer; by the words of invocation; by the repetition of the Gloria; in and through the preaching; by words of dismissal and benediction.

What has happened in and through the Liturgical Movement?

What kinds of changes and revival have we witnessed in recent years?

6. *Music and dance*

Study the place of music and dance in most religious acts in primitive cultures, and in biblical times.

The place of music and dance in church worship of the third and fourth centuries A.D., the pruning of both under the Puritans and why. Cf. Erik Routley's *Music of Christian Hymnody*, pp. 49–54 for the Puritan discipline of psalmody. N.B. The contribution of J. S. Bach, Bourgeois, Geneva, etc.

The revival of music and its contribution to worship, especially the Masses by great composers, Oratorios, the tremendous impetus to hymn singing given by the Wesleys, the place of organs and choirs in cathedral worship (organ and choral scholarships to Oxford and Cambridge Universities). Are cathedral choir schools and organs in their latter days?

Listen to records of modern folk masses, Singing Nuns, Gelineau Psalms, Joystrings, etc.

Which kind of instruments are most helpful to congregational singing?

What kind of music is most suitable for worship: the jingles of the day as William Booth believed (why should the Devil have all the best tunes?); music which is more orthodoxly musical, less easily understood, but much more dignified and enduring; a mixture of all kinds?

Note the gradual re-introduction of dance into worship through forms of dance drama. (Cf. *Against all Reason* by Geoffrey Moorhouse; photo of ex-ballet dancer nun, pp. 178 ff., African sisters dance in worship, p. 144.)

In their *Festivals of Heaven* the Darmstadt Sisters include gracious minuet-style movements as they sing hymns of praise. (A group of young people danced 'Lord of the Dance' down through the nave and into the chancel of Salisbury Cathedral.)

Ask for examples of music and dance in worship from missionaries who work amongst the 'younger churches'.

7. *Customs and folklore*

Study the religious practices of different religions in different countries down through the ages, e.g. Ancient Egyptian, Roman and Greek rites; sects such as the Essenes and Qumran Covenanters; modern religious cults in West Indies and South America; Bantu prophets in South Africa; Kimbanguism in Congo.

Study also the practices of less well-known churches in this country: the Russian and Greek Orthodox churches and their liturgy; the Lutheran and Reformed churches; Dutch Reformed church.

Note first the major differences in religious customs, secondly the common factors, e.g. the initiatory rites or baptismal and purificatory rites; the importance of the cultic meal (very often using bread and wine); the place of sacrifice, human, animal (in primitive worship), votary gifts, self-offering; attempts to appease gods and evil spirits. Similarities in birth, marriage and funeral rites. Why are there these common elements? Look at the way religious beliefs have grown out of folklore: the dying and rising god of Isis and Osiris; incarnation of Dalai Lama of Tibet; early beliefs of Kimbanguists in Congo that Simon Kimbangu would return as the 'Comforter', the Third Person of the Trinity (compare with Montanism).

8. *The modern media*

How have films helped or hindered the desire to worship? Study various examples, e.g. *The Ten Commandments*.

What contribution have radio and television made to the worshipping life of the community in general? Do they meet a need, or mostly antagonise those who have chosen *not* to worship God?

9. *Conclusion*

To what extent does a study of the history of the development of man's worshipping practices and religious beliefs help us to understand our own position and needs?

Note to teachers

The material suggested here presents a fairly comprehensive study of the subject of worship. The teacher may wish to select certain sections only, or divide a class into groups to work and research on separate aspects.

This could be used as a scheme for an integrated studies course where the expertise of geographers, historians, sociologists, music and art specialists would be available. Without the co-operation of other departments it would be impossible to tackle this work.

BIBLICAL THEMES

'THE STONES CRY OUT': THE TEMPLE TELLS ITS OWN STORY

1. *The vision of a Temple*

David dreamed of building a Temple but the final task was not his but his son Solomon's (1 Chronicles 22: 1–13).

We do not always realise our dreams: sometimes ours is the vision and someone else carries it through, e.g. (1) Martin Luther King: 'I have a dream ...'; (2) Prince Albert's vision was only realised in the Royal Albert Hall by order of Queen Victoria *after* his death.

David had made Jerusalem the religious centre as well as the political capital of his people, and had brought the Ark into the city amidst great jubilation, dancing and rejoicing. Study the processional Psalm 24 (perhaps use it for choral reading or dance). Show on a model how the procession would have to 'ascend into the hill of the Lord'. Link this psalm with 'Lift up your heads' from the Messiah, and the processional hymn 'Ye gates lift up your heads ...' used by the Iona Community for the 'carrying in' of bread and wine.

2. *Solomon's building project*
2 Chronicles 2: 7. Study the exact details and proportions of the Temple. Show on a map, with ribbons or arrows, the sources of Solomon's materials, e.g. cedars from Lebanon.

Study the Dedication Ceremony and prayer (in modern version) 1 Kings 8.

3. *The place of vision*
The vision and call of Isaiah (Isaiah 6). Show exactly what was happening in the Temple at the time, and how the actual movements and objects merged into the images of his vision.

4. *The place of renewal*
Centralisation of worship in Jerusalem temple under Josiah (2 Chronicles 34: 1–7). The discovery of the book of law (2 Chronicles 34: 8–22). Josiah's reforms (2 Chronicles 34: 23–33).

5. *The place of destruction*
2 Chronicles 36. Captivity and exile in a strange country. Separated from the Temple there could be no more sacrifices, hence worship became centred in the word of God rather than ritual.

Study Psalm 79 (following the Destruction).

Study Psalm 137 (following the captivity in Babylon).

6. *The rebuilding of the Temple*
The rebuilding under Zerubbabel and the extension by Herod.

Make a model and give dimensions.

Relate to the words of Jesus (Mark 13: 1, 2). Show the good and positive qualities in Herod's character through his building projects.

7. *The place of sacrifice*
Give full details of Temple ritual: the daily sacrifice; special sacrifices such as at the presentation of a child, e.g. Jesus's presentation and circumcision (Luke 2: 21–25); the Day of Atonement ritual; the Passover Sacrifices (ref: *Life in the Time of Jesus* by Margaret Boys).

8. *The place of duty*
Story of the Good Samaritan with background details of why priest and Levite would not stop. The priest's special week of duties at the Temple forbad any ceremonial defilement such as contact with a dead body. Background details of the priestly party (ref. to The Men against Jesus in *The Mind of Jesus* by William Barclay).

The story of Simeon and Anna 'waiting for the consolation of Israel' and a study of the Nunc Dimittis in its original context (Luke 2: 25–39).

9. *The place of learning*
The system of rabbinic schools centred upon the Temple (*Life in the Time of Jesus* by Margaret Boys).

Jesus's visit to the Temple at the age of twelve and his discussions with the learned doctors of law (Luke 2: 40–52).

Paul's student days under Gamaliel (*Life in the Time of Paul* by Margaret Boys).

10. *The place of temptation*
Jesus was tempted in the wilderness to begin his ministry in a sensational fashion by throwing himself from one of the pinnacles of the Temple (Matthew 4: 5–7).

Explain what the pinnacles were, and what they were used for, and why this should have suggested itself as a temptation.

11. *The place of corruption*
The trick questions to Jesus whilst teaching in the Temple during the week before his crucifixion (Mark 11: 27–33; Mark 12: 13–17; Mark 12: 18–27; Mark 12: 28–34).

The following are very suitable for dance drama. The swindling and cheating in the Court of the Gentiles, over-charging and underpaying on the exchange rate to the Jews of the Dispersion who returned for the feasts; the cleansing of the Temple (John 2: 13–22; Mark 11: 15–19).

12. *The place of wholeness*
Peter and John cure the lame man who sat begging at the Gate Beautiful in Solomon's Porch (Acts 3: 1–11).

13. *The place of destruction*
Jesus's predictions of the destruction of the Temple (Mark 13; Matthew 24: 1–31). The actual siege of Jerusalem and destruction of the Temple under Titus Flavius in A.D. 70. (Amount of detail given would vary according to the age of the children.)
(Biblical references have been given for the teacher's own preparation *not* necessarily for class use. This theme should be followed rather as a pageant in which certain episodes in the history of the Temple are highlighted with the teacher filling in the background. Or, again, it is like showing a series of transparencies on one theme: connecting links will be necessary.)

2
TEAM TEACHING
(with special reference to personal relationships)

Anyone emerging from a college of education these days will be familiar with the ideas of team teaching, integrated studies, project work, etc. These methods of discovery and learning are by no means new, and are largely accepted as the most valuable ways of educating children of primary school age. They are not nearly so widely accepted or practised in secondary schools, particularly where courses lead up to G.C.E. examinations.

In the primary school, where a class teacher has his class for most of the day, there is relatively little difficulty in relating all the class studies over a certain period to one centre of interest, and this has for long been the normal approach. When a child enters a secondary school, it must often seem to him that subjects are now self-contained and perhaps even unrelated, since he has specialist subject staff. Usually he enjoys having a variety of teachers instead of the one class teacher, and in this respect school becomes more interesting for a while. Obviously specialist staff in the different subjects are a 'must' in higher education, but primary school teachers must sometimes despair that their efforts to help children see education as a whole are swamped by the approach to learning in the secondary school.

What is the answer? There are obviously no easy solutions when secondary schools are faced with the sheer practical difficulties of lack of space, shortage of staff and inadequate equipment. There must be thousands of teachers who could echo my own experience of having to teach in corridors, gym changing rooms, stationery cupboards, canteens, medical inspection rooms, the prep. rooms between labs. where one contends not only with the practical work going on on either side, but also with a variety of undesirable smells, or the irritating spectacle of hamsters treading their wheels in endless cycles. Years ago, 'Jane Hope'* did a great service to teachers when she publicised visually some of the practical difficulties that we face. Her books were exaggerated, of course, but perhaps few people outside of educational circles realised how slight were the exaggerations.

It is very difficult, in the face of some of these problems, for teachers to sustain the enthusiasm and vision that may have been awakened in their years of training. Nothing is more frustrating than to plan out project work and then find that there have to be last-minute room changes, or the projector you need is needed elsewhere or has broken down, that there is a shortage of sugar paper or card, or that an oral lesson is going on next door which cannot allow for even the normal, healthy noise of group work. However, these problems are known to *all* teachers, not just those in secondary school work.

The problem that is perhaps more peculiar to secondary schools, and in many ways more difficult to overcome (though some of the C.S.E. courses have tried to do this), is that the syllabus for most subjects is geared to examinations. This makes many teachers fearful to experiment with 'fancy' methods which, however stimulating and exciting, might involve a departure from the set course leading to the exams. It is deplorable that in G.C.E. courses we so rarely have time to 'stand and stare', and wonder at the discoveries we are making, and the new scenery we are seeing for the first time. It is often like travelling on an express train where once we have begun the journey we find ourselves whizzing past places we should love to stop and explore at leisure, because we *must* get to our destination by a set time. Often, as teachers, we are filled with real regret that we have to rush along, but we are faced with little alternative. Year after year I have had to say to my 'O' level groups, who have really come alive in some heated discussion, 'We must leave that now and get on: we'll come back to it after the exams are over, when we have time'. There never *is* time, of course, or, at least, there never is a time like the present when the topic has

* Jane Hope, *Don't Do It* (Frederick Muller).

arisen spontaneously and naturally. You cannot really successfully engineer discussions, and often after the exams there is a terrible inertia and sense of anticlimax (which is wholly understandable). The moment has gone, and very often gone for good, when one has had to clamp down on real enquiry and fruitful opposition.

This is not to suggest that meandering, without any real sense of direction or any set goal, is the ideal. Nor is it to suggest that there is no place within R.E. for real scholarship and academic discipline in biblical studies. It is important that for those who wish to study theology at University level, there is a course in schools which gives them sound foundations. It is equally important that in the sixth form, students should not develop a lazy attitude towards the subject, imagining that it requires no effort and no thought. As in all things, one must strive for and achieve a proper balance. It is simply a recognition that the need to cover a certain amount of ground in the two or three years leading up to the examination makes many secondary school specialists more reluctant to make any departures from the set course, or 'sacrifice' any time should another member of staff request some cross-fertilisation of subjects.

It is in just this kind of situation that I feel R.E. has a very real contribution to make. It is not just that R.E. is one of the subjects where this cross-fertilisation can most easily be done: it is one where it cannot properly be avoided.

The educational prophets of this decade all *insist* that Religious Education embraces all education; that religion is concerned with the values and direction of life, and therefore all that is important to full living has a religious connotation. All questions about life are basically religious questions. (As students are so often reminded, even if they opt out of R.E. teaching, they can never avoid the religious questions that children will ask no matter what the subject happens to be. This is perhaps one of the most important reasons for providing an adequate professional course in Divinity in colleges of education in order to ensure that students have faced and thought through some of these questions before they meet them in the classroom itself.)

Perhaps R.E. has the advantage over all other academic disciplines, of being able to say that there are no real boundaries to the subject, but it would be a very foolish R.E. teacher who gave the impression that he was 'poaching' on other territory or 'supplementing' the teaching of other subjects. Yet there are very obvious and natural links with Literature, Art, Music, History, Science, Drama and Dance. With careful planning it is possible to cause common areas of study to coincide: for example the study of the early life of Abraham and the culture from which he came could be taught at the same time as the History Department began the study of the Sumerian civilisation. My History colleagues, in the past, have often been very grateful for the mutual help given when we have found time in R.E. to make ziggurats out of hundreds of matchboxes when time simply would not allow for model-making in their course.

The opportunities for 'coincidence' are fairly limited, however, and depend very much on the goodwill existing between individual members of staff. Even in the face of some of the difficulties mentioned above, it *is* possible even in secondary schools, to relate subjects in such a way that it provides a piece of real team teaching. By team teaching I am not suggesting that subject staff need necessarily combine lessons, though this is sometimes possible and desirable, but rather that a whole area of study should be approached from a number of different angles to give a complete and comprehensive survey.

Those engaged in Environmental Studies often find themselves caught up in a completely natural form of team teaching. History, Geography, Nature Study, Geology, Art and Architecture are all involved in such work, and it is important to recognise that they do come together quite naturally. I suspect that sometimes in project work, everything is *made* to fit in with the project, whether it does so naturally or not. It makes for a nice 'neat' unit of work but its artificiality is not educationally valuable.

One very natural piece of team teaching could arise from the teaching of personal relationships. This topic forms a very important part of many R.E. Syllabuses at present, but it is regrettable that it is often taught in isolation from other departments.

An experiment in team teaching

It had been the policy of our school (a girls' grammar school) to invite 'outside' speakers to come each year and give a series of talks on the subject of Sex Education and Personal Relationships to the third-year girls. Sometimes these were good, sometimes less so, in which case they required a fair bit of 'tidying up' by the R.E. and Biology teachers. After one particularly bad year, the head of the Biology Department and I talked with the Headmistress, and agreed in future to tackle this whole subject between our two Departments. As we mapped out our plans, we began to see that it could be done even more effectively with the co-operation of the Home Economics Department. We called it team teaching, and so it was, but (partly because of the enormous difficulties of rearranging a time table, and partly because it seemed the most satisfactory way of tackling it anyway) we retained our separate lessons each dealing with our particular aspect of the overall theme, but with the set intention of interlocking, overlapping and complementing.

Before we actually launched the project, the Headmistress arranged a meeting for all the parents of those girls involved in the study. Each year we were encouraged by the numbers of parents who did come, but surprised at the 'absences'. We had assumed that, in a subject of such vital importance in which the parents themselves would be so intimately involved, they would be most interested and anxious to know what we planned to do and how we planned to do it. We had hoped for an almost one hundred per cent attendance. For our part, we desperately wanted the assurance of the backing and blessing of the parents as we co-operated with them in this area of their daughters' education. I cannot stress strongly enough the value of such parents' meetings. We launched out on our set course with natural trepidation, but free at least from the fear that we were usurping the parents' role or exceeding our responsibilities, and conscious that this was team teaching not simply between departments within a school, but between the school and home.

In the R.E. lessons, we tried to conduct our particular discussion on personal relationships, within the family, school, general circle of friends and the community as a whole before coming to the question of specific relationships with the opposite sex. It led us to examine the qualities that one looks for in a friend, why some people appear to have few friends; the problems of loneliness; the difference between solitude and loneliness; the problems of jealousy that can arise between friends; the question of the 'right' of parents to exercise influence or even control over the choice of one's friends; some of the tensions within the family created by growing up and the need for growing independence, and the whole question of the balance of freedom and authority (which was viewed particularly from the parents' standpoint). As a basis for our discussions we used Ian Birnie's most helpful book *Encounter* (published by McGraw-Hill), and in the section on 'Growing Self Awareness' we dealt with some of the fairly typical fears and perplexities that loom on the adolescent horizon: feelings of inferiority, moodiness, problems of personal hygiene, fear of not attracting the opposite sex, uncertainty in choice of clothes. We also dealt briefly with the question of masturbation and its frequently accompanying guilt feelings, and, since some young people go to the extreme of thinking it a form of perversion, we went on to define real perversion and mentioned the fact of homosexuality, largely to reduce curiosity and any lurking fears, and to encourage a sympathetic and loving attitude towards such people. In this we related closely to the Biology teaching which by now had dealt with the physical changes taking place in adolescence.

When we came to the section 'Encounter with Love', and the Biology Department had begun to deal with the physical facts of procreation, we spent quite a while discussing what we mean by love, and working out a rule, or a yardstick, with which over and over again we were to measure our actions and reactions to certain situations. The 'yardstick' emerged after a close study of 1 Corinthians 13 and was really a paraphrase of it, though I think many of the girls were unaware of this at first. Having prepared the ground, we were ready to study more closely the questions of ethics and morality that arise in connection with relationships with the opposite sex.

I found the easiest way of tackling this was through the experiences of an imaginary couple, tracing the development of their relationship from the moment they were first attracted to each other through to marriage, the establishing of a home and the welcoming of the first baby. One class chose to call its 'couple' Bonny and Clyde. They discussed why it was that Bonny and Clyde were attracted to each other in the first place (and came to see the falsity of many of the television advertisements). Once the couple had started dating each other regularly, they came to see that it brought a responsibility which does not permit a wilful hurting of each other. Flirting, they decided, was definitely 'not on'. However, they recognised that Bonny and Clyde might well want to terminate their relationship before it became 'too serious', and so we discussed the least painful ways of doing this, applying our yardstick of respect and reverence for the other; our conviction that we should honour and never dishonour.

But since the relationship between this couple continued and deepened, there was naturally an increasing desire to express their affection for each other, and so there came the inevitable question of, 'Petting: how far should you go?' It was interesting to see how strongly the argument on the grounds of fair play appealed to the girls. They were extraordinarily frank in their discussion and mostly agreed that there was a real need for restraint, because it simply wasn't fair to 'lead a boy on' and to impose heavy strains through arousing desires in him which they were not prepared to satisfy fully. They accepted that sex being the necessarily powerful force it is, is not to be used as a plaything.

In our imaginary situation, Bonny and Clyde decided that they were 'in love', and so we distinguished between mere infatuation and real love. This led on to the question of engagement, what it is for, and what factors need to be considered in deciding the length of the engagement period. Some of the girls even went into the matter of the price of engagement rings, and discussed whether or not an engagement ring was necessary.

One of the reasons given for a time of engagement was that it enabled the couple to prepare for marriage in all sorts of ways. Here the Home Economics Department came into its own. In the cookery lessons, the girls learned about nutrition and balanced diets, and how to prepare tasty meals economically. They experimented in planning, cooking and serving a supper party. They were given ideas on how to budget and how to break down the monthly salary cheque or wage packet. They studied differing qualities in linens, curtain fabrics and carpeting. They planned a trousseau, and each girl chose one household topic such as cookers, furniture, gas, kitchen equipment, etc., and made a special study of it.

For the purpose of our discussion we assumed that Bonny and Clyde were not in a position to marry for a while (possibly both were students), but being deeply in love, they faced the question, 'What is wrong with sexual intercourse before marriage?' In the R.E. lessons we tried to see that sexual intercourse is part of the total fusion of two personalities, and to isolate it from its proper context within marriage is to rob it of most of its meaning and much of its enjoyment. We looked at this question from a biblical as well as a commonsensical point of view, and stressed that the conditions need to be absolutely right if intercourse is to be the crowning glory of a man–woman relationship and not just the expression of biological instincts. We put forward the view that there needs to be a sense of permanence and utter security in the relationship (and this is especially important for the woman). There must be a guarantee of privacy and safety from pregnancy, and freedom from guilt, even for engaged couples! Needless to say, there was heated discussion and sharp cleavage of opinion between the girls over this point, but our yardstick reminded us that real love seeks only to give, never to take that which it has no right to have.

Next came the preparation for the wedding. In the Home Economics Department, they looked at designs for wedding dresses, tried out recipes for wedding cakes, worked out the relative cost of a reception and noted special points of etiquette. They even prepared a reception to which they invited the Headmistress and other guests, and photos of which appeared in the school magazine.

In R.E. we considered just what has to be arranged before a wedding can take place either in a church or register office. There was, of course, a fairly heated discussion as to the sort of wedding Bonny and Clyde should have, and we saw just how difficult a decision it can be sometimes. We also looked at some of the problems involved in a 'mixed marriage', in terms of denominationality as well as nationality.

The girls were given a guide as to how to set about getting a mortgage, and many of them went to Building Societies and got their own information. They looked at show flats and building sites, and visited the Ideal Home Exhibition.

Finally Bonny and Clyde married and settled into their new home. In order to keep up mortgage repayments (and possible H.P. agreements) it was decided that Bonny should continue to work. So, naturally, they were not anxious to start a family straightaway. It was at this point that we had a great deal of heart searching. Was it the right time, we wondered, to mention family planning and contraception? We had been offered the loan of an excellent film on this issue by the local health authorities. The staff involved in this teaching examined all the pros and cons, and finally it was decided that we would show the film to the parents and leave them to decide. There was complete agreement amongst those parents present that this should be shown, but we also stipulated that we would follow it with a film on V.D., so that any suggestion that the girls were being given the 'know-how' to avoid pregnancy would be followed by a solemn warning of the dangers of promiscuity. These films were introduced and shown in the Biology lessons and from the very matter-of-fact notes which the girls made afterwards, we were assured that this had been the right age at which to give the information (when it was not an emotional issue). Many of the parents expressed their appreciation and thanks that we had tackled the subject in this way.

When, finally, Bonny and Clyde did 'plan' their family and were expecting their first child, the Biology Department dealt with the various stages of the growth of the foetus and the actual birth, whilst the Home Economics Department gave specific information about the various amenities provided by the Welfare State and the Local Health Service.

Each girl kept a project folder, and many of them were extremely imaginative and well-produced. Excerpts from some of these folders have been included. It is highly probable that in a few years' time, they will be able to turn to them and find them of real help. We are sure that as the girls came to grips with the physical, psychological, emotional, moral and economic factors in human relationships, it has proved a valuable as well as an enjoyable part of their learning for living.

We did not, of course, escape without criticisms. Strangely enough, these did not come from those most closely involved, the girls themselves or their parents. From them we received nothing but encouragement and thanks. Criticisms were levelled at us, however, by people who are not yet aware of the revolution that has taken place within Religious Education and who feel that a theme such as Personal Relationships has no place in the R.E. syllabus. It is surprising how many, even in educational circles, still regard R.E. as a matter of telling Bible stories with suitable explanations and amplifications. Yet, Goldman, Acland, Loukes and others who have researched in this field have shown us so clearly that the R.E. lesson, besides imparting Bible knowledge, provides a right and proper place for the exploring of moral values and their implications for living.

In our team teaching we certainly sought to discover the biblical answers to the moral problems under discussion, but in this kind of teaching, care has to be taken that moral values and religious beliefs are not identified so closely that those young people who are unable, as yet, to accept religious beliefs feel that they are, *ipso facto*, rejecting all moral foundations. However, even though the teaching in these lessons may not be exclusively Christian, it does give the opportunity to explore Christian values in a relevant life context and to recognise them as one set of values that may be considered amongst others.

It is a bewildering world in which young people grow up today, and one in which values are completely topsy-turvy. Even the

Church no longer speaks with a clear voice on some issues. If by our discussions we have helped this group of young people towards a life in which they will find rich, rewarding, satisfying relationships then we are happy that we have helped to give them a religious interpretation of life without which according to the *Spens Report* 'no boy or girl can be counted to be properly educated'.

A summary outline of the course on personal relationships

RELIGIOUS EDUCATION	BIOLOGY	HOME ECONOMICS
1. *Encounter with self*		
The need for friendship.		
What qualities do we look for in a friend?		
The influence of parents in our choice of friends.		
Why are some people lonely?		
The difference between loneliness and solitude.		
Grace to see one's friend preferred to oneself.		
The balance of freedom and authority.		
2. *Encounter with love*		
What does it mean to be attractive?	Personal hygiene.	
What do we mean by love?	The changes taking place, in (a) the boy in puberty (b) the girl in puberty.	
Study of John 15:13. 1 John 4: 18.	The menstrual cycle.	

RELIGIOUS EDUCATION	BIOLOGY	HOME ECONOMICS
1 Corinthians 13.	The need for reproduction.	
Love must always *give* John 3: 16.	Sexual intercourse.	
Bonny and Clyde		
Meeting the boy or girl friend for the first time.		
Dating.		
Flirting and going steady.		
How best to terminate a friendship.		
Petting.		
Engagement: (a) for what? (b) the ring.		The break-down of wage packet.
Sex before marriage?		Nutrition and diet.
The wedding service (a) what sort and where (b) what has to be arranged		Home furnishings and furniture, fabrics, carpets, etc. Visit to Ideal Home
(c) the expense.	Contraception.	Exhibition.
The future home: how to obtain a mortgage.	V.D. Pregnancy and the birth of a baby.	The trousseau, bridal dress and attendants' dresses.
Visit to show flats, houses and building sites.		How to plan a reception. Experimental reception. Local health and Welfare amenities.

A wider piece of team teaching could also involve the Geography and History Departments to help with projects on world poverty:

nutrition in underdeveloped countries, the welfare state as a British attempt to cope with poverty, the specialised agencies as an international effort.

Summary of the course

LIST OF THE BOOKS AND FILMS USED

Books

Encounter by Ian Birnie (McGraw-Hill).
He and She by Kenneth Barnes (Penguin Press).
Facing Life's Challenge by J. Hills Cotterill.
The Everyday Miracle (for the photos) by Lennart Nilsson, Axel Ingelman-Sundberg, Claes Wirsen (Allen Lane, The Penguin Press).
Sixth Day (text book) by John Merrigan (Darton, Longman & Todd).

Films

From Boy to Man, From Girl to Woman (Boulton-Hawker Films Ltd., Hadleigh, Ipswich, Suffolk).
Half a Million Teenagers (V.D.).
To Plan your Family.
To Janet a Son.

(The girls were encouraged to include in their projects any poetry, prose or songs which related to the subject.)

SOME OF THE PROBLEMS INVOLVED IN A COURSE OF THIS NATURE

For those who feel they would like to attempt a course on personal relationships, it may be helpful to share some of the difficulties we met. 'Forewarned is forearmed, etc. . . .'

The whole of our third year followed this course, and I think it would be true to say that, in the main, they all enjoyed it and found it valuable. But in any school within one year group there may be as much as ten or eleven months' difference between the oldest and the youngest. At that age, it makes a great deal of difference. Whilst some still seem to be innocent little girls, others appear to be very grown up, well developed, and fully assured that they know it all. Great care is needed on the one hand to avoid distressing girls who (even today) may be naïvely ignorant, and on the other to give sufficient information to guard them at a time when they are very vulnerable. It is this very need which seems to me to point to the necessity for giving the biological facts within the context of the *total* personal relationships. The emphasis surely should always be on relationship rather than sex.

Some of the older girls may want to air their knowledge in an unhelpful way, and they should be carefully forestalled. The teacher needs a kind of cat-like agility to leap from encouraging freedom of discussion with some to checking attempts to show off with others. One had to be one step ahead all the time, anticipating questions and remarks. Not all girls of this age have boy friends (though the vast majority have), so discussion should be handled in such a way that those girls without boy friends do not feel inadequate and miserable failures. Again, stress upon relationships in their widest context may help to scale down the status symbol importance of a boy friend.

Another difficulty with such a wide age range is that, whilst biological terms and technical vocabulary may be understood by some, for others explanations will be needed. One girl writing of the tensions of adolescence said that it was like being 'straddled across the gap between childhood and adultery'. In another class, this time of second years, we were discussing the Ten Commandments and one girl asked if adultery meant 'pretending to be much more grown up than you really are'.

We were fortunate in that, in our school, the year was divided into groups according to age anyway, rather than being streamed according to ability. So, by and large, the older girls were all in one class and the youngest in another. It was interesting to notice how the two groups varied in their responses and reactions. For the younger group everything seemed to be a clear-cut issue seen in black and white. For the older group there were many greys over which hung big question marks and whilst we tried to lead them to make choices and come to conclusions of their own, they were often very anxious to know what *we* thought was the right thing to do in a given situation.

This raises another issue. Not only may there be problems about the ages of the girls, but possibly of the staff too. The very young members of staff found this course extremely difficult and in a subject where there may be heated discussions discipline is a little precarious. To start with, the classes were sometimes shy and embarrassed, and the first lesson often resembled a bingo hall with every eye down, or a prayer meeting with every head bowed. We found a little sniggering, though not very much, but it is most important that initially the teacher should do most of the talking in a matter of fact way without embarrassment or emotionalism. It always helps if one can add plenty of humorous touches: it relaxes the tension immediately. Obviously an experienced teacher is likely to do this far more easily than someone new to the job, though not always so. The question of personality is important here. Years of training do teach us not to reveal too much in our faces, and we usually master the problem of blushing after a few years in the job. In tackling a course like this an older person will either have been married for some while, probably with children, or if single is less likely to be emotionally involved than a younger person. Often in our team teaching the younger teachers were themselves courting, or were engaged and just about to be married, or were married and expecting their first baby. In one sense, of course, this was a great help as they spoke with the authority of experience, but in other ways it sometimes caused considerable embarrassment. It is possible that a young teacher may not herself have resolved some of the problems that have to be discussed and this would be both difficult for her and unhelpful for the class. Young people are very quick to detect weaknesses and, unless extremely well controlled, can ask very personal questions.

Even an experienced teacher might think it inadvisable to launch into this kind of work until he or she had come to know the class very well and had developed an easy relationship. This was one of the reasons why we felt so strongly that the subject should be tackled by subject staff within the school rather than a visitor who had never met the classes before. Another reason that weighed strongly was that, not infrequently, various personal problems begin to surface for the pupils themselves. Perhaps there are lurking fears and doubts which may be disposed of, or greatly reduced through the lessons. If a teacher has a good relationship with the class and is known to be available, individuals may want to come and talk and ask advice. Sometimes people who are afraid to ask questions in class, and are perhaps ashamed of some ignorance, will seek out the teacher alone. Others may want to talk about family problems, or their older sisters or friends, and often there is quite important follow-up work and counselling. Sometimes the confidences shared can be a very heavy burden to carry and this is perhaps another reason why a course of this nature needs to be conducted by mature (not necessarily older) members of staff.

Dealing with relationships within the family is sometimes like taking the cork out of a bottle labelled 'family moans'. It is not altogether easy to assess how much value there is in letting people air their grievances and have an enormous grumble about the apparent unreasonableness of their parents. There does seem some point in letting them complain enough to see that everyone seems to meet with the same sort of friction, a kind of lowest common denominator. Then, when the initial pressure from removing the cork has eased off, one can try and stand *in loco parentis*, or ask a pupil to do so, and either through role plays or sweet reason, argue the parents' viewpoint. Of course, there are always some who will not really listen and immediately come back with, 'That's all very well but you don't know my parents . . .'

Obviously there has to be some discussion on family relationships if the whole area of personal relationships is to be explored thoroughly, but if such discussion is to be positive and helpful, the teacher will need to keep very tight control of the class and perhaps even to rein it in quite ruthlessly at times. Understandably parents will feel uneasy about family disclosures in class discussions, but often the teacher can be the parents' greatest ally.

I well remember one class which was complaining bitterly because parents always wanted to know where their daughters were going in the evening and what time they would be home, sometimes even insisting on meeting them. They chafed so much at being treated as children (so they thought) that we acted out in a role play the experience of a girl who was given complete liberty. She went to a party. Her parents did not question her movements and showed no interest. When she left home they had no idea where she was going or what time she would be returning. At the end of the party all the other girls were met by their fathers on foot, or were collected in cars and everyone assumed that she had made her own arrangements for getting home. She walked home entirely alone and got in at 1 a.m. No one was waiting up, no 'good night' message was left on the kitchen table with a hot drink prepared. She crawled miserably to her bedroom. Neither of her parents stirred or called out to assure themselves that she was all right. She lay in bed thinking that she could have met with an accident and be lying in a hospital bed, or she could have run away, or she might have been murdered on the way home and her parents would not have had the slightest idea until they found her empty bed in the morning.

Some of the girls were honest enough to admit that if they had been in that girl's shoes they would have been dreadfully upset and would have felt such neglect could only indicate that their parents did not really love them very deeply. Others were quite indignant and were sure no parents would act so irresponsibly, and others began to show that they would feel very sore indeed if their parents did not worry and fuss over them a bit. All at once the class was laughing at itself because it suddenly dawned on them that they were being egged on in their vehement protests against the very things that earlier had been the grounds of their complaint.

Sometimes there has to be a curb placed on the discussions because in team teaching one is working to a schedule which involves other departments, and the timing of their link-up is important. It is good to have plenty of opportunity for class contributions but even so these need to be kept within certain limits or discussions could meander endlessly. It is generally accepted that discussion lessons are amongst the most difficult to handle anyway, and in personal relationships they are no exception.

One point at which we in the R.E. Department felt that we had failed was in not sufficiently justifying moral values on any except religious grounds. Probably because we derived our own moral views largely from our Christian insights and understanding of the nature of God and of man, it was almost impossible to avoid identifying religion and morals too closely. Although some of the arguments put forward seemed fairly convincing in the classroom, I did not feel that they would be strong enough to hold a girl in situations where passions were roused.

Throughout this discussion of team teaching in personal relationships, I have referred to the girls in the school in which I taught and have outlined a possible course for girls. Some of the course might be adaptable for boys but, in the main, I should not imagine that it could be presented in anything like this form to boys of the same age, though many of them need a similar course geared to their growth and interest.

3
DANCE DRAMA

Further fruitful areas of team teaching can be found in the P.E. and R.E. departments in dance drama. For some time now there have been churches which have sought to find a place for drama in their worship, not only to express joy and adoration, but to communicate a vital message in visual statements, though there is still much prejudice to be overcome in this realm. Increasingly in schools, movement has been seen to belong to more than simply the dance lesson within the P.E. curriculum. For years dancing meant the specialised forms of dance such as ballet, ballroom or folk dancing. Free movement in dance drama is a newer development in education which began to emerge about thirty years ago when the Laban method was introduced into schools, and has steadily gained a highly respectable status among educationists.

Perhaps it is not a new development at all, but a rediscovery of a lost part of our culture. Amongst less sophisticated peoples, dance is an important part of any ritual, and spontaneous clapping and dancing are natural, easy and fascinating to watch. Moments of emotional intensity often lead to dance: the joy of a marriage, the pride at an initiation ceremony, the sorrow of a death. Movement is, after all, the most natural way of expressing our feelings. We may be slightly embarrassed at the foot tapping and hand clapping of a Negro congregation, but they are quite simply giving expression to the joy that we so often feel we must stifle for fear of appearing too emotional.

From earliest childhood we use outward gesture and movement to convey our wants and to express our innermost feelings. Often it is unconscious and perhaps even unintentional. We are usually unaware that our walk indicates our mood of despair or joy, our state of exuberance or deep-seated fatigue. Without consciously thinking about it we register our distaste by a wrinkled nose, our disgust by snapping our fingers, our helplessness by a shrug of the shoulders. As children, we literally jump for joy and clap our hands in pleasure, and even adults are not unknown to perform a little jig when excitement and anticipation can no longer be contained.

Growing up (and none of us quite makes it!) is both exciting and bewildering and it brings a need to work out a philosophy of life. The teenager finds welling up within him, all uninvited, the age-old questions that man has always asked: Why am I here?, Who am I?, What is life all about, and where is it leading?, and he feels a desperate need to find answers. He sometimes feels moody, and little wonder! There are strong emotional as well as physical reasons for this. He is often grappling with thoughts and ideas that are so deep that they cannot find form or expression. They are liked blurred images that he cannot quite get into focus, and there is no real peace of mind until they are clear. They will go on struggling for expression until he finds the right medium.

Many of us will remember early attempts to articulate our inner feelings in poetry. We were probably desperately shy in this and perhaps secretly half ashamed at what began to pour forth once we got started. We would have been mortified had anyone got hold of these private revelations and read the secrets of our mind. It is strange how the comparatively few injustices of school life seem to stand out like jagged rocks in the sea of our memories. One such memory for me was an occasion in the upper school when the French master came upon some of my literary efforts, probably inadvertently left in my notebook. With a lip curling with scorn he held it up to the mixed class as though it were rather a nasty smell and proceeded to read the doggerel. If he had slapped me in the face I couldn't have felt more injured or humiliated. In these attempts to articulate thought, the need for expression does not necessarily include the need for communication or sharing. It is a privacy into which no adult should gatecrash.

Some find outlets in art and music, but writing, painting, playing a musical instrument or sculpturing are all forms of expression which require special skills, whereas dance is natural to us all. It can be developed and cultivated in such a way that it becomes a real art form and consequently more satisfying to watch and more releasing to perform. But surely it is true to say that for all of us 'it is in the blood' and that as we abandon ourselves in movement, 'deep down in the subconscious mind mysterious memories of earlier activities of our race mingle with our own conscious behaviour'.*

An example of how dance drama can help young people to externalise and make concrete their inner thinking was given by a class of fifteen-year-old girls who, as a follow-up to several class discussions, decided to present a dance which they called Everyman and his Emotions. The dance begins with Everyman sitting on a raised central platform (in the stance of Rodin's *The Thinker*) contemplating his many and mixed emotions that swirl around his feet like sea mists. He is appalled as he observes how very undesirable, sometimes thoroughly nasty, some of them are and longs to rid himself of depression, greed, hate, pride, etc. He studies each of the emotions in turn as they separately dance before him. To music ranging from Shostakovitch and Stravinsky to Davy Graham and Jethro Tull, he watches generosity, depression, greed, humility, conceit and pride, love and hate, cynicism, joy and jealousy well up from his inner being. He is horrified to discover that the emotions are not necessarily isolated from each other, but are tangled up and intertwined. For example, he has to leap up to try to separate love and hate when hate has a stranglehold on love who, with arms wide open to embrace all, is in a terribly vulnerable position. He watches despairingly as joy, dancing freely and ecstatically with gazelle-like leaps, is suddenly dogged and pulled back by jealousy. At last, no longer satisfied with a passive acceptance of this inner confusion, he makes a deliberate attempt to reject all that is unworthy.

With great slashing and spurning movements he casts aside greed, depression, cynicism, etc., and with drawing and inviting gestures he chooses what is good, and unites himself with them in a total self-offering.

It was in the preliminary class discussions that the girls suddenly

* Bruce and Tooke, *Lord of the Dance.*

came to see how very mixed up we all are, and evolved the idea of love and hate and joy and jealousy dancing together. It was only after those dancing humility had simpered and giggled their way around the stage several times that it emerged that they thought being humble meant being embarrassed. In fact, humility was one of the hardest emotions to dance. After clearing up the first misunderstanding, the girls had to be dissuaded from presenting nothing but a series of bowing and scraping movements. It provided an opportunity for explaining that true humility means accepting ourselves in a realistic way and acknowledging our strengths as well as our weaknesses. A tremendous amount of incidental teaching took place as the groups worked out their separate parts of the dance and tried to think their way into their particular emotion.

The final presentation was of a high standard and was presented very movingly, but this would have been impossible had the dance specialist in the school not joined the R.E. specialist in what became a real piece of team teaching. The girls themselves became very enthusiastic and even up to the last rehearsal were producing new and exciting ideas. Undoubtedly the primary value of this dance was in what it did for the dancers themselves by giving not only new insights but also expression to things dimly understood.

Dance, whilst it may be a creative way of giving expression to scarcely formed thoughts and ideas, can also be a very telling way of communicating to others. Movement is nearly always informative. Even in the world of nature, the bees are able to give accurate information to each other as to the whereabouts of nectar simply by the type of movements made. Just as bees seem to understand the language of movement instinctively, so do we. We know very quickly if art or music appeal to our aesthetic senses, but we need to be educated in our understanding of them. Dance has the power to make immediate contact, and the education needed in dance is more along the lines of performance than understanding. Some quite elderly people, who themselves would have had absolutely no experience of this kind of dance in schools, have been overwhelmingly appreciative of its powerfulness to speak. Even on stage, there are times when the playwright expects his actors to convey a meaning through a gesture, a movement or a look, which speak volumes more than any words.

More and more R.E. specialists have become aware of the tremendous value of dance as a means of expression and communication in this field. This is not to suggest that dance is always a means to an end. As an art form it is an end in itself and its sheer beauty may be enjoyed for its own sake. But as with other art forms, one of its values is its ability to communicate. Would *West Side Story* have made the impact it did through words alone? Or even through words and music?

Through dance young people are able to empathise with others in a positive way. Young people today are greatly concerned by the enormity of the human problems confronting our contemporary society. Even in the primary school they are deeply aware of the hunger, loneliness, hopelessness and incurable illnesses of those around them. They really do sorrow for those affected by tidal waves, earthquakes, avalanches, etc. They care deeply about their own contemporaries caught up in the drug scene. Sometimes the flood of information that comes pouring out from the television screens and newspapers overwhelms them. It's all happening around them now and yet they are so powerless to do anything, or at least the little they can do seems pathetically small in the face of the vastness of the problem. In many schools there is an outlet for their concern through social service activities (of which more will be said in a later chapter), but feelings of sympathy, grief at the horror of it all for others, are stirred up and often leave the young people in a state of unhappiness.

Dance provides a most valuable opportunity of sharing and demonstrating the plight of the lonely and the poor and the hungry, of really entering into their experience without actually being those so afflicted. Since in R.E. we deliberately encourage a concern about those in need and try to arouse positive sympathy, should we not perhaps take greater care to see that there are *many* kinds of outlets for expressing this sympathy? Dance could well be one. Themes such as war and peace, racial conflict, freedom and authority have been the subject of many dance dramas in and out of R.E. lessons.

Then, too, it is a powerful way of helping classes really to understand a biblical story and get inside the experience of the characters. Take, for example, the incident where Ananias goes to Saul the persecutor after his conversion to encourage him in his new-found faith and to give back his sight. Following that, he took Saul to meet his fellow Christians in Damascus. One could try to get a class to understand how the Christians must have felt and reacted to Paul's admission to the Church by sending two of the class out of the room, to re-enter after a few minutes as Ananias and the newly-converted Paul. Ananias would have to make the necessary introductions and explanations to the rest of the class playing the part of the Church. Granted that children are not always sufficiently uninhibited to present extempore drama it was astonishing how, when this was once tried, so few in the class could think of anything to *say*. They knew how they felt but couldn't express it verbally. Imagine this scene in dance, however. The devastating entry of the persecutor, the recoiling in horror of most of the Christians, the attempts to run away, the pleadings of Ananias and then of Paul and the gradual acceptance of him into the group. With very little prompting I think this same class would have been able to put the whole tense situation into movement in a way that would have given them rich insights into the feelings of both the Church and Paul.

In one attempt to team teach with the dance specialist, a fourth-year group of girls worked out a mime dance on the Last Supper and Gethsemane. Some may well imagine that, in introducing dance drama, the amount of time spent in organising and staging the dance would be out of all proportion to its teaching value. Let me assure you that this need not be so. This particular fourth-year group worked on their chosen subject hoping that it might ultimately culminate in a dance, but it took five or six lessons of learning about and discussing the event before ever any movement was introduced. In all there were only about four or five rehearsals before it was given as a public performance. By far the major amount of time in this piece of work was spent in trying to understand why Jesus was in such agony in the garden. Within the framework of the whole passion we discussed the sinlessness of

Jesus and the intolerable burden that one's own sin can be, let alone the whole weight of the world's sin. We thought of his natural human shrinking from physical pain, his sense of desertion by the disciples (and yet their wholly understandable fatigue), but far more the sense of separation from God that this 'cup' would bring. We tried to grasp exactly why the Cross had to be, and what the work of Christ was. It was a real grappling with the doctrine of the atonement at a fourth-year level. In order to mime the Last Supper, we had to go over the various stages of the passover feast (revision of second-year work) and try to enter into the feelings of Jesus towards Judas in particular, and see what exactly it was that he was instituting in the new covenant. What was it that he was trying to say to the disciples through these visual symbols, and what do bread and wine say to us today? Having thought and talked about it, we finally began expressing some of this thinking in movement with considerable help from the dance specialist. The agonising and wrestling of Christ on the slopes of the Mount of Olives (built up with movable blocks) was so moving that some of the parents who came to watch shed tears. During the Gethsemane scene we had no music as the girls felt that it would be more effective to have the sound of heartbeats represented on a drum. As the mental agony and spiritual anguish of Jesus increased, so the drumming would grow louder and faster, and as he reached the point of submission, so the heartbeats would calm down and revert to a normal, regular rhythm, till finally there would be absolute silence. Then, after a dramatic pause, the armed men led by Judas would arrive and the beats would be those of marching. (In order to be able to make these changes and let the beats follow the movement rather than vice versa, we used a drum rather than a record or a tape of heartbeats.) In all, the dance only lasted about ten minutes, but I would hazard a guess that those girls will never hear the passion story read again without memories being awakened, just as the thousands of visitors who saw the Oberammergau passion play will never fail to remember it each Easter.

4
DRAMA

At one time the annual nativity play or passion drama was a highlight in what might have seemed the dull routine of R.E. lessons. Indeed, to watch any play or, better still, to take part in a play was a great event in school life. Now we are teaching children who see plays, sometimes even a succession of plays in one evening, every day of their lives. Does this mean that the medium of drama is no longer effective or is very much less so? Are children becoming immune to the power of drama to communicate?

Far from having exhausted its usefulness and purpose in the classroom, it is even more necessary since it can provide opportunities for active participation rather than the often passive response evoked by television. Sometimes teachers bemoan the lethargy and apparent lack of imaginative ideas amongst young people, and wonder why this condition is so prevalent. Is it perhaps because so little has been left to the imagination, that, no longer exercised regularly, it has become sluggish and inactive?

Some argue that one of the reasons for the increased interest in witchcraft and the occult amongst adults today is that much of the mystique of life has been removed. Science seems to have answers for everything; there are few mysteries, and yet the human heart yearns after an experience of the numinous, the 'mysterium tremendum', and if it doesn't seek it in and through the living God, it will often seek it by 'picking the lock' of the spirit world.

The need to act

At one time, before television became a commonplace in every home, children relied much more on acting out all sorts of ideas in their play. They formed gangs and secret societies and went to war with each other; they were Red Indians and Cowboys; they were spies moving secretly amongst the enemy; they performed heroic deeds and enjoyed imaginary adventures, and often the apparent detachment of a child was due to the fact that he was acting out a role other than his real one, in a fantasy world. It was a form of pleasurable escape for the child brought up in the drabness of slum areas, or a world of companionship for the only child. But it is much more than this. Think how important it is for children to explore and discover through this natural medium of play acting. It is a means of extending knowledge and sharing in the varied experiences of other people.

I knew of one quite small child who, in the 1940s, spent an entire Easter holiday punting up and down the half-mile lake in the grounds of the home to which she was evacuated in Somerset. Surrounded by thick woods, the lake was a marvellous setting for innumerable adventures and she, with another evacuee, transformed the banks into all the great seaports of the world. Five minutes punting downstream would land them in places full of Eastern promise. At the next landing stage they were in Amazonia being chased by head hunters through the woods. They tramped from the east coast of Africa to the west through the equatorial jungles, facing all the hazards of snakes, crocodiles and all manner of wild beasts with a superb courage. Even meals became a tiresome interruption to their escapades.

The groom of the house gave the little girl an old saddle which she fixed to a horizontal branch of a tree in the orchard, and perched in that saddle she rode for miles to faraway exciting places, meeting with incredible adventures and fascinating people—all the time within calling distance of the house.

One day (during a phase when she was reading of the explorations by canoe of a Scout troop) she decided to 'paddle downriver' in search of adventure. Dressed in a borrowed scout uniform and an old pair of boots given her by a great aunt, she ventured out into a country lane where she began to lash out furiously with her imaginary paddle. As she rounded a bend in the road the adventure was rudely interrupted by the appearance of an elderly lady with her dog. A look of mingled astonishment and panic spread across the old lady's face at the extraordinary sight. How could she possibly have known that her presence had temporarily smashed a moment of spine-chilling thrills?

We have all made this kind of identification to a greater or lesser degree in our childhood following the reading of a book, the watching of a film or some other stimulus that started the train of thought and left us to continue it in our imagination.

Nowadays it seems that children have neither as much chance nor as much desire to make these experiences their own in play; because the stimuli are so numerous all energy and time is needed for absorbing them. If it is generally true (and it certainly is in particular cases that I have observed) that children spend a far greater proportion of their leisure time in passive watching rather than active play, then this must have a deadening effect upon the imagination. Perhaps so much has been given to us these days through visual media that the imaginative faculties have been lulled to sleep, or have never been allowed to develop. A surfeit of visual aid may have left some children in such a state of bewilderment and saturation that they have 'switched off' their imagination. They are no more able to cope than the child who is swamped by too many new toys at Christmas, and who after having played with each of them in turn for a while, turns to a simple but familiar piece of wood or rag which offers him a kind of security. For true creativity of thought there must be the time for absorbing new ideas through such media as films, radio, television, and adequate time for the working out of those ideas in a concrete way (since children rarely think in abstracts) until they become part of one's own experience.

The outward and concrete sign of an inward and abstract concept

The first reason then that might be given for the place of drama in R.E. is that it provides an opportunity for children to realise in concrete situations some of the quite difficult concepts with which they have been struggling in the R.E. lesson. 'Loving one's neighbour' presented considerable problems to the learned men of Jesus's day. We cannot expect it to do less today, especially when the neighbour turns out to be one's enemy. But this concept put into a real-life setting and acted out begins to make sense, and sometimes quite unwittingly young people produce their own version of the Good Samaritan. For example, a group of 'bovver' boys turned up at a young people's Sunday afternoon rally which was being held on church premises. Most of the young people were church members or regular churchgoers, the 'bovver' boys were members of a local youth club. The speaker at the rally wondered quite how his plans for the afternoon could include them. They were to discuss the theme of responsibility and then divide into groups to work out some way in which they could present their thinking on the subject within the context of worship at the evening service. The speaker quite expected that the 'bovver' boys would walk out when he explained what was wanted, but they didn't. Instead, they went off into the minister's vestry. Some time later he went to see how they were getting on. The boys were sitting around with their feet up on the vestry table, the air was absolutely thick with smoke. But they had been working to some purpose and had produced a role play which featured their club. The fellow on the door was beaten up by some thugs from another club and robbed of that night's takings. Several club members in turn arrived and the role play was a study of their reactions. Two simply stepped over the unconscious doorman, another ran away. Finally, a member of a rival club, passing by, saw the situation and came in and rendered first aid and called the police—all of which was the responsibility of the unfortunate fellow's own club members, and they had failed him. The 'bovver boys', who had expressed a desire to contribute something to the evening service though they weren't going to 'do anything religious', had, in fact, presented a profound religious truth in their own terms.

The value of identification

Then, too, drama is valuable in the R.E. lesson because it enables children to identify themselves with positive qualities such as courage, meekness, endurance, care and concern for others. It is important for them in the formulating of value judgements that they work out their position in imaginary situations before being faced with the real ones. For example, within a piece of classroom drama or a role play, they may have to decide whether or not to stand out against the crowd or their gang in order to maintain truth. Never an easy thing to do, it may become more of a real possibility if they have already faced up to the problems of 'going against the stream' in another setting. This kind of dramatic medium is one of the best ways of imparting moral values, for instead of saying 'this is right' and 'that is wrong', which may at once stiffen resistance, the class is encouraged to make the discovery for themselves. The art of teaching at this point is to produce the kind of situations in drama which will challenge the children to ask the right questions, and to distinguish clearly positive and negative qualities, and what in the end is of lasting rather than fleeting value. In the follow-up the teacher needs great mental agility and resourcefulness to steer and guide the discussion to some fruitful end rather than let it deteriorate into uninformed waffle. 'We are all entitled to our own opinion' is frequently heard in R.E. lessons, but the teacher needs to show kindly and humbly that even though this is so, not all opinions are of equal worth since not all opinions are sufficiently informed or guided by altruistic motives. It is immensely difficult to allow great freedom of speech in a lesson, and yet show young people that having declared their position they may not have said all, nor arrived at a particularly satisfactory conclusion. At least, it is always necessary to handle this kind of lesson firmly so that it produces positive results, without the teacher appearing to have all the answers or seeming to steam roller over the views of the class. Throughout, there needs to be a sense of mutual sharing, and this is not just an act that has to be put on. It is indeed a learning process for all, and many teachers would confirm that often they have come away from a lesson the richer for the insights given them by their pupils. I quote from a letter from a very humble school chaplain: 'On the whole the girls teach me far more than I teach them . . .'

A most useful book which shows how role plays may be used as starters for discussion is *Creeds and Controversies* by P. E. Miller and K. S. Pound (E.U.P.), already in use in many schools. One value of the role plays in this book is that they can be adapted to different age-groups, though they are intended for the senior part of the secondary school. At the end of this chapter there will be suggested ideas for other role plays and spontaneous classroom drama which will encourage identification with what is 'true, honourable, just, pure, lovely and of good report'.

An effective research method

A further argument for drama in R.E. is that it can be a most useful and interesting form of research. In order to produce a piece of drama there is first the need to sift out the relevant and important facts, and, since it was rarely the concern of the biblical writers to elaborate on the facts, there is the need to fill out with background detail, and this should send pupils scuttling off to the library to search for the necessary information. At times it may enable pupils to learn certain biblical passages as part of the play (without asking them to memorise chunks of the Bible for no apparent reason), or if the actual scriptural words are not used, they will need to sit down and think through them carefully in order to produce their own contemporary version. Sometimes this exercise leads to an important grasp of the underlying truth.

Of course, in drama one has to be prepared for all eventualities and sometimes the children's version of a story highlights the inadequacy of our teaching. The story is told of an infant school class which was to present a nativity play. Every child in the class was to take part, and all the parents were invited to form the audience. Everything went relatively smoothly in rehearsal except for the reticence of one small boy who was unusually shy. In order that he should not be burdened with too large a speaking part, he was invited to be the innkeeper. The only words he had to speak were 'I'm sorry but there's no room at the inn'. Each time the play reached this point, either the innkeeper seized up or burst into tears. It seemed as though he would never be able to say his one and only line. 'I don't want to tell Mary and Joseph that there's no room for them,' he sobbed. On the afternoon of the performance, the teacher wondered greatly how things would go when the play reached the crucial point where Mary and Joseph arrived at the inn. When it came the innkeeper remained silent for a moment, then his lip began to quiver, and the teacher feared the worst. Then the child was heard to say, 'I'm sorry there's no room at the inn—but do come in and have a drink'. Full marks to the innkeeper for not violating his own integrity!

Another story is told of a class (more than familiar with strong language) that was dramatising the story of John the Baptist. The child dancing the part of Salome had greatly pleased Herod who asked what she would like as a reward.

'I should like the head of John the Baptist chopped off and brought to me on a dish,' she said.

Herod turned to one of his soldiers and said in deep, dramatic tones, 'Go: and fetch the bloody head.'

The child came back with the Headmistress.

Not only does this kind of research work give invaluable information on background detail, but it often means that the pupils can get behind the events to the real character of a person and his underlying thinking. If, for instance, a senior class were working out some form of passion drama, sooner or later they would have to weigh up the various motives attributed to Judas for his betrayal. It might well be that they would not reach a common verdict, but it would certainly be a useful exercise.

So often this is quite the natural way by which a class gets beyond the superficial knowledge of the facts to a deep understanding of the real heart of the matter. I suppose most people remember 'doing Paul's missionary journeys' at some stage in the secondary school. It may well be that it remains a jumbled memory of maps and riots and long speeches, the importance of which was always a little difficult to grasp. But it is much more important to know something of the character of the man, and the significance of his message, than the particular route he happened to take through Asia Minor. It is such a pity in this area of study to concentrate on the journeys and miss out much of the essential teaching. It is also possible to introduce certain points of biblical criticism in a simple and digestible way through drama. A suggested idea in the form of *This is your Life* programme on the lines of the television series, is included at the end of this chapter. In this, reference is made to such points as the purpose and destination of the book of Romans, the authorship of Hebrews, the lost ending of Mark's gospel, and the reasons for John Mark's turning back from Perga.

There are many very good and helpful filmstrips available to illustrate the R.E. lesson, but it can be an even more memorable form of learning to get a class to make its own filmstrip. Here again it means research into background material, an ability to think of the story or situation in visual terms, and a grasp of the underlying problems not always stated explicitly in the narrative. One such useful experiment was carried out by thirteen-year-old girls on the story of Hosea's domestic tragedy. Many syllabuses very advisedly suggest the teaching of the eighth-century prophets in the third-year course of the secondary school. It is an age when social justice and human problems are very much to the fore in their thinking and usually it is a section of the third-year work that really comes alive since it is easy to show the relevance of the prophets' teaching to twentieth-century living. Having studied the story of Hosea and the way in which he reached new insights about the love of God through his own enduring love for Gomer despite her unfaithfulness, the class set about filming this story in a contemporary setting. The flat in the Home Economics Department became the home of the couple and the film began with all the happiness of their wedding reception surrounded by the gifts of various friends. The girls even made their own wedding cake from tiered cardboard boxes painted white, supported on Smartie tubes and iced with Polyfilla rosettes and decorations. The effect was quite realistic. Younger brothers and sisters were brought in to play the parts of Jezreel, Lo-Ammi and Lo-Ruhamah. Shots of Gomer leaving her home (with a farewell message to Hosea on the coffee table) and a clandestine meeting with her fancy boy in his flashy sports car, were followed by Hosea's discovery of the note, his shock, hurt, bewilderment, and somewhat unsuccessful attempts to cope with the housework, shown by a sinkful of dirty dishes and an untidy lounge. Even the small children managed to produce pathetic 'Where's Mummy?' looks, though these were quite fortuitous and were only captured through the quick thinking and acting of the girl photographer. Then came a series of shots showing Hosea's search: at the local station as the rush-hour crowds pour out past the ticket barrier, at the launderette, in a Chinese restaurant, at a bistro, at the police station where he studies the Missing Persons' list. Finally, in their interpretation, he catches up with Gomer when she appears before the magistrates' court, and is heavily fined and utterly deserted by other fancy men. The final shots show Hosea having paid the heavy fine himself out of his savings, leading her out of the magistrates' court and reuniting her with the children in their own home again.

The girls worked out the ideas for themselves and did all their own filming, sometimes without any supervision. There were technical errors in the photography, of course, but in the main it was extraordinarily good. They wrote and taped a commentary to go with the filmstrip and were delighted to show it to other forms in the school, and their parents at a parents' evening. The value of this is obvious in that they related the story and teaching of Hosea to a modern day situation, and did so with considerable sympathy, enthusiasm and initiative. The added value of the filmstrip method was that their discoveries could be shared with many others, and also provided a means of enjoyable revision when they came to look at it again at a later date.

Such dramatisation is informative not simply because the teaching has been presented in visual terms, but because the pupils themselves have to do the research work and are actually engaged in the presentation, entering into the experiences of those they portray in a meaningful way.

An aid to understanding festivals of the Christian year and other religions

It is sometimes quite difficult to arouse interest and show the importance in Christian thinking of the seasons of the Church's year and some of its ceremonies. Christmas and Easter are well and truly recognised because they spell HOLIDAY, Whitsun, too, until the recent change in date of the spring public holiday. Other occasions such as All Saints' Day, Ascension Day, Advent Sunday, etc., are often forgotten. Yet could it not be very helpful, in our virtually pagan environment, at least to keep the ideas and purpose of these occasions alive in the thinking of young people? It would need to be done, however, in a very imaginative and attractive way if it is to capture interest and produce understanding. For some who never attend church, it might be of real educational (as well as spiritual) value to explain the ordinary Sunday by Sunday activities and at least outline what happens at a service of Holy Communion, a baptism, or marriage, and give simple explanations of the meaning behind the outward ceremony. Certainly much information of this sort is made available to the public these days through Sunday television programmes, but those who find no place for worship in their lives are prone to switch off anyway when a service comes on. It might even be a useful link-up with local clergy and ministers to get their co-operation in giving 'demonstrations' with commentaries on various ceremonies of the Church. There are problems here in that, in L.E.A. schools at any rate, no teaching with a denominational bias is permitted, so that if this were planned, there would have to be a balance provided by a series of demonstrations representing different types of services. It might possibly be argued that children would find this confusing. With the younger age ranges this would certainly be true. But with older classes it is different. Confusion exists and we cannot always shield young people from the truth. Perhaps ultimately this kind of study amongst young people would lead to better understanding and relationships in the future between different branches of the Church, since there would be less prejudice and fear due to ignorance and distortions of the truth.

Since we are in a multi-racial society and seek to encourage young people today to live in sympathy, tolerance and understanding with each other whatever the creed or colour, it would surely be right and mutually helpful if the Moslem, Buddhist or Hindu children were given opportunities to describe and show the importance of some of their religious festivals, especially since it would help to explain their absence from school on occasions.

It is certainly very valuable to an understanding of biblical teaching if there is a real knowledge of the Jewish festivals. There are many books that describe these very clearly, some of which are included in the bibliography, but with first- and second-year secondary pupils, it is not always very easy to visualise what happens and capture something of the atmosphere. In a study of the background to the gospels, including the religious festivals, I have found it most useful actually to conduct a passover feast in the classroom. On several occasions there have been Jewish pupils in the class and I have approched it very carefully lest it should cause offence. In each case, however, they and their parents have been delighted that this was going to be done and have given immense help. (In some areas, of course, it would be relatively easy to enlist the help of a rabbi.) In these celebrations stress was always laid upon the fact that, whilst the lesson was to be entirely enjoyable, it *is* a very special and sacred occasion to the Jews and therefore had to be conducted with great reverence. Each time the classes responded very well and once the preparations were completed, the feasts always went through smoothly and with great dignity. Full details as to how to prepare the food, and, even more important, how to prepare the class beforehand, are included in this chapter, together with an order of service specially adapted to fit into a forty-minute lesson. In order to complete the feast in one lesson, *all* the preparations and explanations need to be done previously, and each member of the class should have a copy of the order of service.

Having shared such a feast in the classroom, the biblical references to the passover and especially to the Last Supper are infinitely more meaningful. Such an experience also provides a natural link and way into some teaching on Holy Communion, the meal of the New Covenant which in the Christian Church has replaced the passover of the Jewish faith.

A way of illuminating Church history

If it is true that the peak moments in Church life can be made more meaningful through drama, it is also true that some of the great turning points in Church history come to life when acted out. A very simple script picking out some of the main points in the Arian controversy and finally winding up in the Council of Nicaea where important points of doctrine were introduced, ended in the speech fading out as a choir took up and sang the Nicene Creed. For those members of the class who were communicant members of the Anglican Church, the Nicene Creed ceased to be quite the mystery it had been before and for the non-churchgoers the unfamiliar language of the liturgy began to have meaning.

A dramatisation of the experiences of Luther leading up to his stand before the Diet of Worms ('Here I stand, I can do no other') not only presented some of the facts of the Reformation, but helped to illuminate some of the current theological thinking, and gave rise to a study of the hymns of the Reformation.

It takes considerable ingenuity to present not simply the facts of Church history but an interpretation of the facts in dramatic form, and it would seem that sadly this is a neglected part of the R.E. syllabus. It is fairly straightforward to give dramatic presentations of the Reformers, and early pioneer missionaries, even of those who in more recent times have taken bold stands against Nazism or Communism, where there is excitement and action. But, the earlier part of Church history is also important and frequently packed with chills and thrills. So often the only visual presentation that some children have of the early Christian era is through epics such as *Ben Hur* and *The Robe*.

Erik Routley's little book, *The Wisdom of the Fathers* (S.C.M. Press) gives most entertainingly and vividly much colourful information which may be used when writing scripts for simple classroom presentations of the early fathers. Such attempts should, however, be scripted (with a narrator and miming cast, or recorded on tape with sound effects, or with words memorised) rather than be allowed the freedom of spontaneous and extempore drama which may lead to garbled and distorted facts.

So, then, the early controversies in the Church and some of the very colourful figures of the first four centuries may provide subject matter for drama, as well as the lives of some of the later great saints, Church leaders, prophets, mystics and preachers. The building of great cathedrals, and the founding of schools, hospitals and religious communities (cf. *West Riding Syllabus*, pp. 46–58) may profitably be taught through the medium of drama as is well known from broadcasts for schools where this is a favourite technique.

The period of modern Church history (1840 onwards) now included as part of the London University A level R.K. examination, covers such exciting movements as the Christian socialist movement, the Tractarian movement, the modern missionary movement, the ecumenical movement, not to mention the many ways in which the nonconformist conscience and social reform made themselves felt. It is not always easy to enthuse one's students with a sense of the adventurous spirit of that era, largely because most of the names, facts and figures are entirely new to them. But clothe the facts in the shape of drama and events begin to live and become exciting.

The plea, then, is that visual expression work should not be reserved simply for the junior and middle school age-groups. It has an important place in the education of the older age-groups, and it is not impossible to combine this kind of presentation with examination courses.

General value of drama

These then are some of the considerations to be borne in mind as we bring drama to the R.E. lesson as 'the handmaid of the Lord'.

And, of course, all the reasons for encouraging drama of any sort also apply to drama in R.E.: the fact that it is fun, and learning *should* be fun; that it encourages co-operation and teamwork, and the development of aesthetic senses through movement, art, music, design, etc. In fact, many of the reasons given for the place of dance drama in R.E. apply to drama, but drama includes the need for verbalisation, creative writing and the ability to carry out background study and research. Feelings and emotions are largely portrayed in dance, whereas additional reasoning can be portrayed in drama.

Summary of the chapter

THE VALUE OF DRAMA

1. It is a natural, necessary and valuable way of acting out ideas as they are absorbed, thus grasping them, quickening them to new life, and making them our own before they slip away from us.
2. It is an important and meaningful way of exploring profound religious truths and concepts (possibly reached through R.E.) in concrete terms that match our experience.
3. It is a means of identification with what is good and positive, thus helping us forward in the making of our own value judgements.
4. It encourages research into background material, into the underlying teaching not always explicit in the event recorded, and into ways of presenting it in a relevant life context.
5. The main purpose of some forms of drama is to give information, e.g. about ceremonials, feasts, sacraments and special festivals of Christian, Jewish and perhaps other faiths; or to present the dry bones of Church history in an exciting way.
6. It has all the value in the R.E. lesson of drama anywhere, i.e. the fun it brings, the teamwork it promotes, the stimulation of the imagination, the thrill of performing and of giving pleasure to others, the development of aesthetic tastes, etc.

FURTHER IDEAS

1. *Role plays*

These are very useful starters to class discussion, and may be 'staged' spontaneously or pre-arranged on tape. Very often no props are needed and space is not a major problem since they can take the form of a conversation or dialogue. Sometimes there is a need for more action, but it is rarely that a role play cannot be enacted in a classroom.

One of the most valuable ways of using the role play is to create an imaginary situation (such as the club scene above) and have different people acting out their responses to that situation, so that the *whole* class is involved in watching, assessing, choosing and sorting out what action it would take. In questions of social and ethical values it invariably sparks off a lively discussion. The following are examples of the kind of situations that could be the subject of role plays:

1. An old lady has collapsed on the pavement just as the bus, for which you have been waiting half an hour, appears. You have an urgent appointment for which already you are slightly late, and there are few other people around. What do you do?
2. The bus conductor has not taken your fares and you near the stop where you intend to get off. The conductor goes upstairs as you ring the bell. What would you do?
   Suggest that different people act out different roles so that the class is faced with the choice, e.g.:
   (a) Getting off without paying?
   (b) Giving the fare to someone else to hand to the conductor?
   (c) Sending the fare to the bus company later?
   (d) Accepting that the conductor has only himself to blame for not doing his job properly, and giving the money to charity?
3. Your closest friend confides in you that she is either pregnant or on drugs. What would you do, if anything? What are the different steps possible?
4. You receive a number of anonymous letters. What is your attitude and how would you act?

5. You have seen some juniors from your school shoplifting in a local shop. What would you do about it, if anything?
6. An immigrant family comes to live next door. They seem to keep themselves very much to themselves. How do you show your neighbourliness? What would you do if at first you were rebuffed?
7. If you found a father shouting angrily and beating his small son, with a daughter standing by sobbing her heart out, how would you act and react? Include all the problems involved in this sort of situation.
8. After a test, a teacher has carelessly left the remainder of a packet of file paper on her desk. What should be done? Discuss the different possibilities and whether or not the element of stealing comes in if the paper is kept, or even distributed round the class, but used for school work.
9. Small amounts of money have disappeared from people's purses from time to time in your form. What do you feel would be the best steps to take for all concerned? (Let members of the class act out the part of class members as well as teachers.)
10. You hear that the mother or father of someone in your form has died. How would you try to show your sympathy?
11. You see someone deliberately setting a booby trap in the Chemistry Lab. that is likely to be a fire risk. How would you act?
12. A friend of yours has told a whopping great lie to get out of trouble. You can see that this lie is likely to lead to others. In principle you don't approve of lying but you also have a loyalty to your friend. What is the best course of action here?
13. Someone has got hold of some pornographic pictures and is circulating them round the class. Your curiosity urges you to have a look, your better judgement tells you not to. Everybody else is in on this. Would you be different from the crowd?
14. Your best friend is deliberately doing bad work in Maths because he hates the Maths master. Would you back him up in this or try to persuade him otherwise?

2. *Readings and mime*

Sometimes it is not very easy to dramatise a scene, either because of stage difficulties, or the amount of time required for learning words and rehearsing. It is quite effective, however, to have the actions mimed or presented in tableau form (needing only a minimum of rehearsal) with a narrator or number of readers giving the story.

It is possible to present Job 1 in this way: a magnificent chapter for choral reading with speakers taking the parts of the different characters, whilst the messengers come to Job in a steady succession miming their parts only. The chapter lends itself very easily to variety of tempo, and is sometimes a useful reading for assembly if the theme is to be suffering.

Scenes from the lives of saints may be presented in this way too, so that, put together, they present a form of pageant.

One church in Surrey presented the *Prayers of Life* by Michel Quoist in this way with two readers for the 'Lord' and 'my Son', and groups dancing and miming the situations reflected in the prayers. Sometimes this was enhanced by transparencies thrown on to a screen behind the mimers, so that there were moving, real-life pictures of hunger, homelessness, loneliness, etc.

Psalm 24 is another biblical passage that may be presented most vividly in mime and choral reading. In this kind of dramatic happening the discreet use of music is most effective.

A girl in a secondary school once chose to read the story of creation to the background of part of *The Planets* by Gustav Holst, and did so with great dramatic effect, giving sufficient light and shade to her voice, and using pauses sensitively. She held the school spellbound. Professional actors such as John Stuart Anderson have also shown how gripping this technique can be.

3. *Song writing*

A further idea, though not strictly drama, which is creative and fits in best here is that of writing songs on the various topics under discussion. With the prevailing love of folk and pop music, there is considerable scope in this medium. Songs of protest and songs expressing bewilderment at human problems have been popularised by many of the groups, and the precedent is there if young people can be encouraged to write both words and music. For younger classes this is perhaps too daunting a task but they will sometimes write their own words to a current hit tune.

One group that was doing a study of the Scribes and Pharisees wrote a remarkable song to the tune of Bonny and Clyde. Another girl, in the heyday of the Seekers, wrote a hymn in praise of God which ended:

> But if I should lose your love God
> I don't know what I'd do
> For I know I'd never find—another You.

4. *Simulated television and radio programmes*

Just occasionally there is real justification for taking the format of a B.B.C. programme and using this structure to get across some teaching points, e.g.:

What's my Line? to illustrate trades in Palestine in the time of our Lord.

Call my Bluff, University Challenge, Just a Minute: to test general knowledge of particular biblical sections covered, or of the facts and figures of some present-day social and economic problems.

Any Questions (and Any Answers), Brains Trust: for the airing of views on current social problems and topical issues (though the representatives of the class should be chosen for the fact that they will bring *informed* opinions and viewpoints).

It is not a wholly acceptable technique and has only limited teaching value, but its advantage lies in the fact that the structures are already familiar to most people and therefore only the content needs to be worked out. It occasionally provides a bit of light relief, and it would be unrealistic to pretend that teachers are not glad of such strategies at the end of term, or when they feel 'off colour', or when lessons are likely to be interrupted by medical inspections or fire drill. It is perhaps particularly useful as an occasional form of practical expression for those classes who bitterly resent written work in this compulsory subject, or for less academic pupils for whom written work is so difficult that it slows up the course with the danger of quenching interest.

PRACTICAL SUGGESTIONS AND POSSIBLE DIFFICULTIES

Drama would be far more widely and frequently used in R.E. if it did not entail so many practical and organisational difficulties. There is the problem of space and noise, and also lack of time if one is following an examination course.

Many of the suggested dramatic happenings in this chapter need little or no rehearsal, and others can be prepared effectively in a very short time and still achieve the desired goal.

Role plays need very little preparation, and usually a minimum of space.

The simulated television and radio programmes may often be staged round a conference table, in front of a microphone (real or imaginary). For some programmes it is a good idea to construct a framework representing a television screen and stage the action within that framework thus setting certain limits on movement. This is by no means ideal, but it is a case of adapting to the classroom conditions that exist.

The Church history scenarios may need something rather more elaborate (possibly the school hall), but some of the ideas could be acted out in the classroom, or alternatively recorded on tape as 'radio' plays.

None of these suggestions should prove unduly noisy and consequently disturbing to other classes.

It would be unfair and quite unrealistic to suppose that the organisation of classroom drama is straightforward and easy, but it makes for much less strain and wear and tear on the teacher if he establishes a certain routine which *must* be followed. They are simple but necessary rules.

The cast elected by the class or teacher must be given instructions, ideas and suggestions in the plenary session of the class. If the teacher gives his attention to that one group, the others are likely to become restive.

No one should initiate any movement of desks or chairs without direction from the teacher. In fact, it needs to be understood that any upheaval within the classroom is like a military operation and can have only one commander and one set of orders which must be obeyed promptly.

The teacher needs to have a clear plan of action before starting any removals so that only a limited amount of time is lost, and noise is kept to a minimum.

In planning the lesson *enough* time must be allowed at the beginning and end of the lesson for the organisational chores. The occasions when pandemonium breaks out are when the teacher has run over time and allowed the drama to go on right up to the bell. Then he is left to clear up with children gathering books together for the next lesson, and another class and teacher champing outside in ill-concealed fury because their lesson has been delayed.

During any drama lesson it is important to give the whole class a sense of active participation. This does not necessarily mean that everyone must have a part, though with younger children or retarded or E.S.N. classes it is an advantage to include everyone if it is a practical possibility. Sometimes, however, the cast must be limited to accord with the available accommodation and the proximity of the other classrooms. One young teacher with only a limited experience of dramatic activities in the classroom, having told the story of Eliezer's search for a wife for Isaac, decided to dramatise it. The main characters were chosen, and all those without speaking parts were told that they could be camels in the camel train. Working in pairs to form the camel with a third child mounted on their backs, the train made its way up and down the aisles between the desks. There were the seeds of some good drama there, and the class enjoyed a hilarious lesson, but it made it quite impossible for the Commercial class on the other side of the quad to continue its shorthand dictation because that teacher's voice was drowned by the gales of laughter.

A serious problem to be faced is that of the pupil who somehow slides out of doing any work in these dramatic projects. He takes no vocal part, and refuses to throw in his lot with the script writers or critics. Somehow, such pupils must be encouraged to take their share in what, after all, is a *class* effort, and not a form of entertainment provided by a few for the masses. If it is an obstreperous or indolent member of the class, then a job must be found that will really keep him on his toes. He may be appointed chief technician and given some quite tricky job such as sitting at the controls of the tape recorder (if he can be trusted that far), or stage-managing the cast behind the television screen, or chief photographer, or prompter—any job which will not permit his attention to wander and which will give him a sense of his importance in the total success of the undertaking.

If the refusal to participate is due to shyness, then every encouragement and praise must be given and a job allocated such as 'wardrobe mistress' in a play requiring dressing up, or scorer in quiz games, or chief observer of the audience reaction.

Others not taking main speaking parts can be encouraged to provide appropriate off-stage noises; to look for certain points (suggested by the teacher) as though they were to write columns in a class newspaper as art, music or drama critics. Others could be asked to listen to a recorded play on tape (or simulated as a radio play from behind a screen) and suggest how this could be transposed into visual terms by writing down stage and screen instructions. Those with a greater literary bent could be asked to suggest improvements in the language: ways of making it more colourful, or more powerful, points where a different choice of words would give them greater clarity, or where speeches should be shortened. Classes are quite accustomed to taking notes whilst watching films or slides in science and geography. They can be encouraged to do the same in religious drama.

Certainly whilst drama can and should be enjoyed for its own sake, in the R. E. lesson it should act as a stepping stone to deeper understanding of some biblical story, life of a saint, or moral, social or ethical issues. It needs to be followed by further discussion and/or criticism, and suggestions for practical applications. It should, in fact, become a real talking point that leads on to positive conclusions or value judgements, to a sense of the needs of others requiring some kind of action, to personal commitment, to belief or to identification with some cause.

There is, of course, always the problem of how much time should and could be allotted to this kind of activity when one is following a course leading up to examinations. If the G.C.E. O level course is being covered in a year, the answer is that probably no time can be spared. It may not always fit in advantageously to sixth form exam courses, but role plays and discussion panels might well be used in sixth form general groups. However, the dramatic projects suggested in this chapter would perhaps most usefully find a place in the last two years of the junior school and the first four years of the secondary school course, giving real gain and insight in knowledge and insignificant loss or distraction from the set syllabus. In fact, there is every possibility that it would encourage deeper understanding, greater interest, and more energetic participation in this subject. However, we must accept that here, as in all ventures, discretion is needed in deciding how much of this sort of work can be done and how often. It is all too easy to harbour a bee in one's bonnet and enthusiasm for this particular activity could mean that the time spent in organisation and rehearsal is wholly disproportionate to its lasting value.

Scripts with practical advice which may prove useful classroom material

THIS IS YOUR LIFE—ST. PAUL

St. Paul's missionary journeys feature as a part of most R.E. syllabuses for the secondary school. They *can* be an exciting section of the second- or third-year work, but often they are not. The geographical details, and the many new and strange names seem to prove too much for those (and in R.E. there are often quite a number) who are not prepared to make much effort to understand and absorb what is being taught. Moreover, it is all too easy to teach the journeys as exciting narrative without showing their relevance to young people today, or conveying the vision that motivated Paul's actions or kept him 'pressing on' through sickness, peril, shipwreck and all manner of dangers.

The use of the biblical material in this form of *This is your Life* programme (and it is but one of many possible ways of introducing the topic), is intended to show the kind of man Paul was, and the things he most surely believed, rather than to give a full and comprehensive outline of his journeys (not that one can get a full outline even by reconstructing his life from the Acts and Epistles).

A certain amount of licence has been used in an attempt to make the account come alive, and some of the allusions will need amplification by the teacher. It can be easily adapted or abbreviated for different age-groups. The teacher might well feel it wisest to act as Question Master and so ensure that the programme 'hangs together'. His experience will enable him to fill in any awkward gaps between the introduction of new characters. Each contributor to the programme speaks his opening sentence off-stage or behind a screen, and then makes his entrance. In each case, Paul should look suitably surprised and delighted and greet his visitor accordingly. Full details of what he actually says in greeting are not always given in the script: these can be made spontaneously.

If the programme is conducted in one sitting without pauses for amplification or explanation, it should take approximately fifty minutes.

There are twenty-one characters including the Question Master and they enter in the following order:

Question Master
Ananias
Barnabas
John Mark
Lois and Eunice
Silas
Lydia
Philippian Jailer
Aquila and Priscilla
Silversmith 1
Silversmith 2
Paul's Nephew
Agrippa and Bernice
Luke
Centurion
Publius
Roman Christian
Roman Guard

It may not be possible to do the whole programme in one lesson, in which case it is possibly best to make a cut after the exit of Lydia and the Jailer.

THIS IS YOUR LIFE

OPENING SENTENCE (*off-stage*): 'Brother Saul—the Lord has sent me . . .'

Enter ANANIAS

QUESTION MASTER: Ananias, you were the first Christian to brave meeting Paul after the extraordinary happenings on the Damascus Road. How did you know the Lord was calling you to go to see him?

ANANIAS: I suppose it was just a bit of sanctified imagination. All Damascus was running with the rumour that the great Saul, scholar and persecutor of the Church, had journeyed to Damascus especially to root out all the Christians and take them back in chains to Jerusalem. But the soldiers who came with him spread an incredible story about some incident that happened three days' journey out, and as I was pondering it that night, just before saying my prayers, it suddenly hit me that the events as they told them had all the stamp of a genuine encounter with our risen Lord and that Saul was now probably a converted man. Well, as I prayed I kept thinking of a man at the other side of the city, sitting in isolation and in a desperate plight. If Christ had really stopped him from carrying out the mission on which he'd come, what was he going to do? He could hardly just go back to Jerusalem. I thought of his loneliness, his blindness and the *desperate* longing he must have to be assured that all his previous persecuting of the Church had been forgiven both by the Lord himself and the Christians. The more I thought about it—putting myself into his shoes—the more I felt I'd got to go to see him and try to give him that assurance . . . So I went.

QUESTION MASTER: Were you scared?

ANANIAS: Scared? I was absolutely petrified—and dared not tell my wife or she would have put her foot down. But even though my knees felt like jelly, I had a strange conviction that I was obeying, so I had to do the other thing too—*trust*.

QUESTION MASTER: And of course we know that you went on and that Paul received not only assurance of forgiveness but his sight as well. (*To Paul*) What did it feel like as you got your sight back, Paul?

PAUL: Very queer. I could only see dimly at first—but then it got better and better. It was like going through a series of glass doors down a long corridor and seeing the room at the far end more clearly each time I passed through one. I've heard that shock and emotional disturbance can do this to an optic nerve.

QUESTION MASTER: Has it ever happened to you again?

PAUL: No, but it left a permanent weakness. I've always had trouble with my eyes since.

QUESTION MASTER (*to Ananias*): Did you have much difficulty in persuading the other Christians to accept Paul?

ANANIAS: Yes, a great deal. But then many of them had suffered from his persecutions. You couldn't wonder.

QUESTION MASTER (*to Paul*): Why did you change your name to Paul?

PAUL: I had begun a new life as a Christian and wanted to show that I was now a new creature in Christ and taking a new name symbolised a new nature. Paul seemed a very good name because it means 'little' and that's just what I am.

QUESTION MASTER: Well, thank you, Ananias. We shall see you again later.

OPENING SENTENCE: 'Hello, Mercury, this is Jupiter calling.'

Enter BARNABAS

PAUL (*exclaims*): *Barnabas*, Barnabas, my dear old friend!

QUESTION MASTER: Well, no study of your life, Paul, would be complete without bringing Barnabas into it. But we were a bit worried about it, wondering if relationships would still be a bit strained, but we can see that they're not!

BARNABAS: Good gracious, no! Whatever differences there have been in the past are forgotten now. Anyway, they were only differences of emphasis and policy. I don't think that deep down we have ever lost our affection for one another. After all, you can't work as a team and live through the sort of experiences we had without feeling indissolubly linked to a person, whatever might happen later on!

QUESTION MASTER: Obviously there is *much* that could be said and if we let you two start reminiscing we'd be here all night. Barnabas, can you tell us of one really outstanding experience that you shared on this first missionary journey?

BARNABAS: I think the memory I treasure most is not a riot or scene with any of the Jewish groups. It was after our disappointment at John Mark leaving us when Paul and I were left on our own to face that terrible journey from Perga to Antioch in Pisidia. It meant travelling along treacherous roads where bandits were very common. Paul had had a bad attack of malaria at Perga and he was really in no fit state to travel, but the muggy heat of Perga was about the worst type of climate for malaria, so we had to press on to higher ground. In that journey I learned a lot about Paul, and what it is that makes him tick. One night when he was raging with fever, he kept crying out in a queer hollow kind of voice, 'Woe is me if I preach not the Gospel'. And although he was a very sick man, this was the thing which seemed to burn him up. I saw something of the driving force behind him and when we prayed together, I found that I had as companion not only a fiery little preacher, but someone who was a mystic as well. On a number of occasions we felt transported into a seventh heaven and frequently when we were on our own, Paul would pass from common language to a kind of exalted, ecstatic utterance, but he only did this when we were alone. And strangely because we were in such harmony, I knew what he was trying to say.

QUESTION MASTER: Well, thank you for telling us that, Barnabas, because that is something we don't get in the official account of your missionary journeys. Tell me, the two of you, if you had your time over again, would you act differently over the John Mark incident?

PAUL AND BARNABAS: It's difficult to say.

BARNABAS: I can't say: one can't put the clocks back. All we can say is that God overruled even in that, and as a result the mission of the Church was even more widespread.

QUESTION MASTER: Well, thank you very much, Barnabas. Reference has already been made to the so-called failure of John Mark, but that wasn't the last you saw of him, was it?

OPENING SENTENCE: 'Look out, Paul, there's a rat right behind you!'

Enter JOHN MARK

QUESTION MASTER: What was the reference to the rat?

JOHN MARK: I was with Paul in his imprisonment in Rome. It's true he was under a kind of house arrest, but they were pretty squalid quarters. And Paul was busy dictating a letter one night when suddenly I saw a movement and yelled to him to stand still—he always paced up and down when dictating letters. I managed to pick up a stick and stun the creature and get it outside. Paul had enough fevers without having bubonic plague to add to them.

QUESTION MASTER: John Mark, when you were a young fellow, what attracted you to Paul?

JOHN MARK: His terrific enthusiasm and energy, the all or nothing outlook that he had to the Gospel.

QUESTION MASTER: What made you give up on that first jouney, then?

JOHN MARK: You are touching on a tender subject, but really it was a number of things:

Firstly, I was plain homesick. I had never been away from Jerusalem before and the comfortable home my mother kept there. I hadn't been used to roughing it and sleeping out, and eating food at very infrequent intervals. Quite honestly, I missed my creature comforts.

Secondly, I had started out with huge enthusiasm and admiration for Paul, but not with a great deal of conviction. At least, not the sort of conviction that would make you do a crazy thing like travel through such dangerous regions unarmed. Nothing could shake Paul, or shake Paul's faith, but then he had had such a shattering experience on the Damascus Road. I had a vague kind of belief, but it wasn't sure belief founded on certainty. That came later.

QUESTION MASTER: Did you resent Paul's leadership over your Uncle Barnabas?

JOHN MARK: *No.* I know this was rumoured at the time, but there's no truth in it. I know my Uncle Barnabas was a much quieter man than Paul, but he exercised as great a ministry in many ways, not least of all in propping up Paul when he felt down and ministering to him through his constant illnesses.

QUESTION MASTER (*to Paul*): Whatever regrets and disappointments John Mark caused you in the first place, I gather these are all healed now?

PAUL: Oh, yes, all rifts are completely healed now. I'm very proud of John Mark, he's like a son to me. He's even thinking of writing an account of the life and teaching of Jesus, more or less based on Peter's preaching, aren't you, John?

JOHN MARK: Yes. Actually I'd finished the outline and started work on it, but I lost the ending, so I'm having to re-draft it. But it should be finished soon.

QUESTION MASTER: Two people who don't get much mention, but who played an important part in the story are two Lystran Christians.

OPENING SENTENCE: 'I don't think there are any bones broken, but put a cold compress on that dreadful bruise on his forehead.'

Enter LOIS *and* EUNICE

QUESTION MASTER: Two people who rendered first aid to you on one occasion.

PAUL: Lois, Eunice! (Greetings all round.)

QUESTION MASTER (*to Lois and Eunice*): Would you tell us briefly what happened on this occasion?

LOIS: Paul and Barnabas came to us from Antioch in Pisidia and Iconium. In both places they had met with opposition and real hostility, so they shook the dust of those towns from their sandals and pressed on to Lystra. Their policy was to move on and tackle fresh areas rather than stay and suffer early martyrdom.

EUNICE: There was a fever of excitement in our city after Paul had performed a healing miracle and we were all speculating as to who this wonder-worker might be. As you know, there is a legend that one of our gods came to us in mortal form once, and only an old couple received him and made him welcome. Ruin came to the city and total destruction except for the old couple, and when they died two cyprus trees sprang up to commemorate them. I suppose it is because of this that our people have always feared that they might again fail to recognise the gods in mortal guise.

LOIS: So, someone started the rumour and soon everyone was rushing about shouting, 'The gods are come down in the likeness of men'. They called Barnabas Jupiter because he was the taller and more imposing-looking figure, and Paul was called Mercury because he seemed a fiery little man who got around at a remarkably speedy rate.

EUNICE: Then people started preparing the altars and getting the oxen ready for a sacrifice; everyone gathered in the square, and began to garland Jupiter and Mercury. Our dialect is a bit

A dance mime of Gethsemane by girls of Wallington High School.

The betrayal scene from the dance mime of Gethsemane.

The dance drama of Everyman and his emotions by girls of Wallington High School.

Finishing touches to a mosaic depicting the Nativity at Kesgrave modern school, near Ipswich.

Robert Parsons painting an Egyptian fresco in the corridors of his school at Portslade, Sussex.

Exterior of a synagogue.

Model of a Mediterranean sailing ship by a student teacher.

Exterior of a Palestinian home.

Interior of the same model.

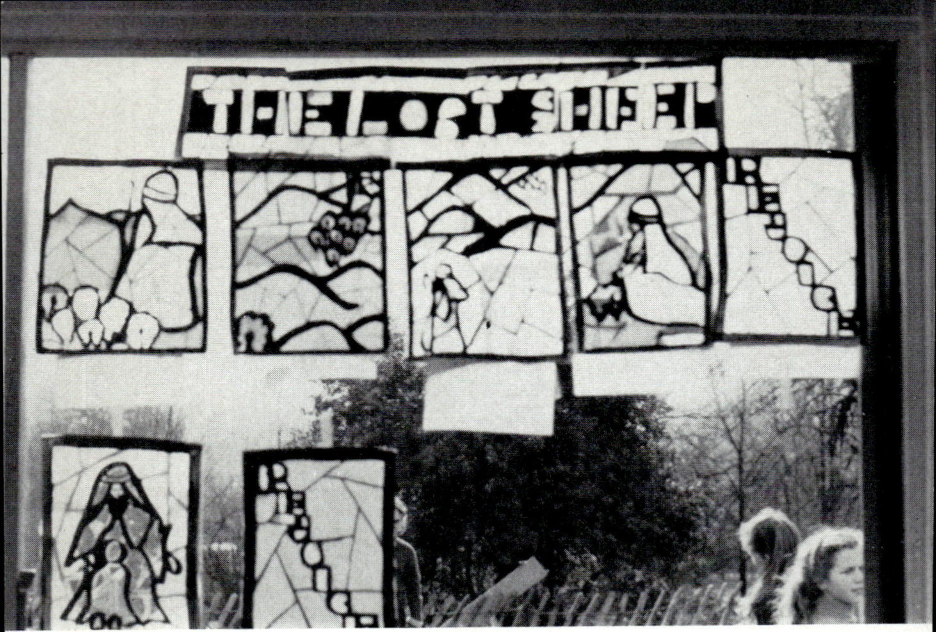

Stained glass windows by nine-year-olds depicting (*above*) the Parables of The Lost Sheep, and (*below*) The Lost Coin.

Scenes from the filmstrip of the story of Hosea by girls of Wallington High School; (*above*) the wedding, Hosea and Gomer, and (*below*) Hosea and Gomer with Lo-ruhamah and Lo-ammi.

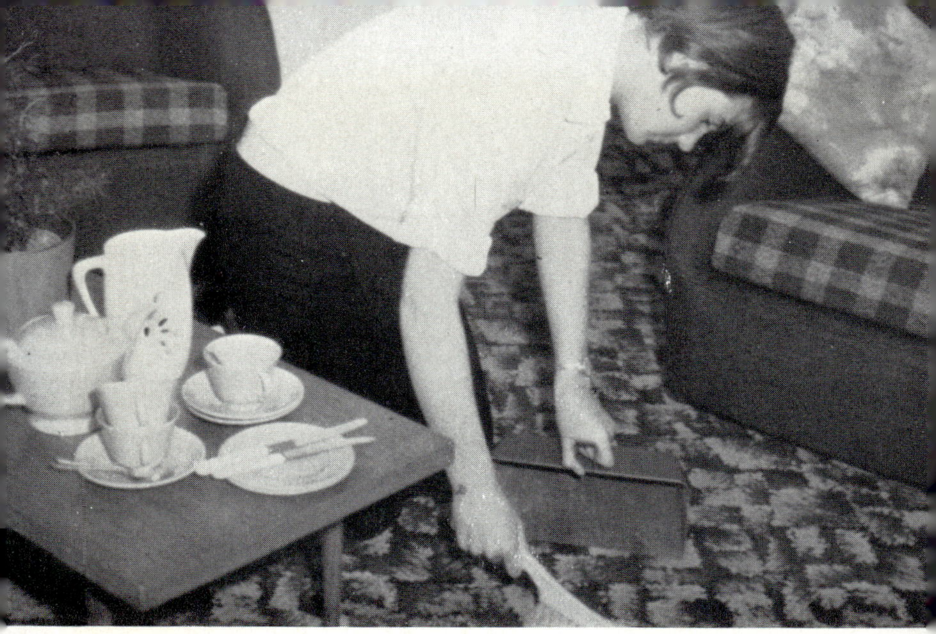

Deserted by Gomer, Hosea (*above*) copes with household chores. (*Below*) Among the many places that he searches for his wife, he tries the station.

difficult to understand at first, especially when it is babbled in great excitement, and it was a little while before Paul and Barnabas realised what was happening, but when they did, they were horrified!

LOIS: Paul yelled at everyone to stop the preparations and vehemently protested that they were only ordinary men who had come to tell us about the true God. People quietened down a bit to listen but it was pretty difficult because the crowds had been nearly hysterical.

EUNICE: And then some men, visitors to our town, but we discovered afterwards that they were Jews from Antioch who had followed Paul and Barnabas, began to whip up the frenzy again by calling out 'Cheats! Deceivers! Liars! ... you deliberately led us on! ... you've just come here to make fools of us ... You have blasphemed against our gods and mocked them! ...' And in no time at all, the frenzied excitement had turned into frenzied fury and, of course, in a crowd like that, mob violence is almost inevitable.

LOIS: Some of us managed to drag Barnabas down a side street and hide him on the roof of a house, covering him with sacking, but Paul was surrounded by such a crowd, we couldn't get near him. People were particularly angry with him because he had started it all by healing the lame man in our city. They dragged him beyond the city walls and I thought they would lynch him, but they started stoning him. That gave us a clue as to who was behind it all, for stoning is the *Jewish* form of execution, not ours! These Jews had deliberately incited this attack upon Paul.

EUNICE: We felt unutterably miserable because we were powerless to help him. When we heard the crowds coming back, shouting that he was dead, we bided our time, and then went to recover his body. But to our joy, he was not dead but unconscious. He was terribly bruised and battered, but mercifully there were no broken bones. We did all we could to ease the pain and make him comfortable, but do you know, in a couple of days he was off, walking to Derbe! It must have been agony for him but he wouldn't stay because he felt his presence in our home was a danger to all of us and so he insisted on leaving. He had astounding courage and endurance!

QUESTION MASTER: And was that the last time you saw him?

LOIS: Oh, no. We saw him on his return visit . . .

QUESTION MASTER: You mean he came back? After that treatment?

EUNICE: Oh, yes, nothing daunted Paul. And then on his second journey with Silas they came and whisked off Timothy who was just seventeen years old at the time.

QUESTION MASTER: Did you feel sore about this?

LOIS: Sore? Gracious no: after all we owe him, under God, our very life. Through his preaching we were born again of the Holy Spirit.

EUNICE: No, *we* couldn't go gadding round Asia Minor with Paul ourselves, though we were dying to tell others of our faith, but we gave Timothy to him instead.

OPENING SENTENCE: 'Keep going, Paul—Cramp in the leg need not cramp your style when it comes to singing hymns of praise.'

Enter SILAS

QUESTION MASTER: Silas, you accompanied Paul through the very exciting events of his second missionary journey?

SILAS: Yes.

QUESTION MASTER: To what were you referring when you spoke of cramp?

SILAS: It was during our visit to Philippi. We were unjustly accused of causing a disturbance (Paul had healed a demented girl) and, without warning, we were flogged and thrown into prison. We were both terribly sore, literally, and were then fastened into the stocks and stuck in that position all night. All round us we could hear others moaning and cursing, and poor Paul got terrible cramp in his legs so that he wanted to scream with the pain, but we managed to convert our desire to scream into a shout of praise and hallelujah. We sang all the hymns we could remember right up to midnight. Then after that, everything happened very quickly. There was a terrific rumble and everything shook violently, and this was followed by the roar of falling masonry. We were jolted out of the stocks but not hurt any more than originally.

QUESTION MASTER: What happened to the other prisoners?

SILAS: Oddly enough they didn't escape straight away, probably too stunned. Then Paul persuaded them to stay put and earn themselves a good conduct report rather than try to make a break when there was so much hubbub outside and no one could be sure if the roads were blocked. The jailer was about to commit suicide: you know the fate of a chap who loses a prisoner in the Roman set-up. Paul called out to him not to do himself a mischief because we were all present and correct. So he leapt into the cell over a broken-down door and stood trembling before Paul, and counted the heads as if in a daze.

QUESTION MASTER: This incident led to his conversion, didn't it?

PAUL: Yes, it was a wonderful and genuine conversion, not one made through fear of judgement. He was a remarkable man in many ways. Do you remember how he got us out of prison?

SILAS: Do I remember? I shall never forget. The praetors sent some lictors to get us out and Paul wouldn't go. He demanded that the praetors come themselves and personally escort us from the prison. When they heard we were Roman citizens they were terribly scared and came and released us, even though it made them look utter fools, and Paul made them give us a public apology. Their faces were a real picture!

QUESTION MASTER: Well, no doubt you could regale us with

endless stories of your adventures on that journey, but we must move on. (*To Paul*) You still have a fairly clear image of the jailer at Philippi, have you?

PAUL: Of course I have.

QUESTION MASTER: Well, we have persuaded two of your friends from Philippi to come here tonight.

Enter LYDIA *and* PHILIPPIAN JAILER

LYDIA: How are you, Paul? Are the eyes giving much trouble?

PAUL: Not too much.

JAILER: (Greets Paul warmly.)

QUESTION MASTER: Now, Lydia, you were Paul's first convert at Philippi, weren't you?

LYDIA: Yes, I was. Paul and Silas had come through the city under the viaduct and were walking along the road which runs parallel to the river where a group of us who were purple dyers were working. They stopped and started chatting to us and they told us why they were in Philippi. As they talked about this new faith, we were absolutely fascinated. They came several times, and I knew that I had found the truth.

QUESTION MASTER: Do you mean that they just came and nattered to you down by the riverside?

LYDIA: Yes, a lot of his personal evangelism was done by chatting to people as he travelled around.

QUESTION MASTER: And you were then baptised in that same river, weren't you?

LYDIA: Yes I was, and there were other converts later.

QUESTION MASTER: What happened in the incident with the demented girl that Paul healed?

LYDIA: She was a most unfortunate girl. She had powers of reading people's fortunes and was an absolute gold mine to her owners (she was a slave), but they worked her to death. She seemed to have uncanny insight and twigged that Paul and Silas were men of God. She embarrassed them terribly by running round after them calling out, 'These men are servants of the Most High God'. Eventually Paul fixed her with an almost hypnotic stare and commanded the demon to leave her. She just gave a fearful shriek and then became perfectly rational and calm, like any of us. But of course it led to an uproar with her owners and this is what eventually led to the imprisonment of Paul and Silas. The owners of this girl made real trouble for them.

JAILER: Of course, when they were handed over to me I had no idea why they were really being imprisoned. I was simply told that they had incited a revolution and were troublemakers known to many cities of Asia.

QUESTION MASTER: Were you impressed by their conduct in prison?

JAILER: At first I thought they were absolute nut-cases, but as the night wore on and I heard not one murmur or grumble about the injustice of their case, not one complaint about their discomfort, I became deeply aware that these men were very different from our usual clients. I'd *never* heard people singing in the stocks before, especially after a flogging.

QUESTION MASTER: So this witness, through their behaviour, had begun to make an impression and raise questions in your mind before the earthquake incident?

JAILER: Oh, yes. A Christian who has learned to be content with his lot and is never found grumbling makes a terrifically deep impression on those around him. But if he *is* a grumbler, he counteracts all the professions of faith that he may make.

Lydia and Jailer leave

QUESTION MASTER: Further on in your journey you came to Thessalonica and Athens, and then went on to Corinth where you soon found new friends.

OPENING SENTENCE: 'You need the warp and woof in Church life as well as in weaving.'

Enter AQUILA *and* PRISCILLA *and greet* PAUL

QUESTION MASTER: How did you meet up with Paul?

AQUILA: Paul came to our weavers' shop to ask for work. We accepted him and, in fact, gave him lodging in our house. He hadn't been with us five minutes before he steered the conversation round to the Gospel. It didn't seem fanatical, but it was like the mainspring of a watch in him. Whatever subject we discussed, somehow or other we eventually got back to the faith, because for Paul everything began and ended in his faith. The whole of his life was related to it, so there wasn't anything we could discuss that didn't ultimately lead back to Christ. Both Priscilla and I began to feel ourselves drawn to this faith which could give a man such deep personal conviction.

PRISCILLA: You can't have a missionary in the home for long without hearing about his faith and his work. Paul seemed consumed with a burning passion to share his faith with others. We'd never met *anyone* like that before.

QUESTION MASTER: Have you met any since?

PRISCILLA: A few, but alas only a few. People don't seem to get so 'lit up' these days and they don't just talk about their faith as Paul used to. They get embarrassed and put on a specially pious voice, and don't speak as though it was the most important and natural thing in the world.

QUESTION MASTER: Priscilla, how did you and Paul get on? We hear that Paul was not much in favour of women taking an active part in the life of the Church?

PRISCILLA (*laughing*): Oh, we had one or two arguments about this, and Paul was so genuinely astonished to find anyone holding a different view from his that it was almost funny, though quite a number of women did get rather upset by his attitude. But my very real affection for him made me careful not to flaunt my viewpoint too much. In fact, I'll let you into a secret . . . *when I wrote the Letter to the Hebrews, I didn't allow my name to be attached to it lest it should offend Paul. But it has given me a lot of amusement to listen to people speculating about its author, never guessing that it was a woman.

QUESTION MASTER: What did you think of Paul's missionary methods? You were in close touch with him over a fairly lengthy period of time, weren't you?

AQUILA: He didn't really have a method, at least not one that would be recognisable, though he could plan a campaign with military strategy when he wanted to. But he just lived the Gospel; he ate, slept and talked it every day. He often wrote letters to churches exalting Christ and imparting spiritual wisdom, but he himself was like a *living letter* with the Gospel written all over him.

QUESTION MASTER: Well, thank you, both of you.

Exit AQUILA *and* PRISCILLA

QUESTION MASTER: On your third journey you met further trouble.

OPENING SENTENCE: 'Great is Diana of the Ephesians!'

Enter SILVERSMITHS

SILVERSMITH I: You probably won't remember us, but we revolted against your preaching because you were destroying our trade.

PAUL: I remember you perfectly well, and I remember that cry, too.

QUESTION MASTER: Tell us briefly what happened.

SILVERSMITH I: Paul began preaching about the Christian God

* The author of Hebrews is unknown, but one fairly serious theory is that Priscilla wrote it.

who had made himself known to men through Jesus, his Son, and every one seemed to find it so attractive they gave up worshipping the goddess Diana.

SILVERSMITH 2: And when they gave up worshipping Diana, they stopped buying our little statues that we made of her. We used to turn out hundreds of them and could never meet the demand. All of a sudden we were left with all these wretched images on our hands. We were doing a roaring trade till Paul came along.

SILVERSMITH 1: But in the end we had to admit defeat. He was preaching to people all through the lunch hour break in the burning heat, in a stuffy old gymnasium that he had rented. Well, we realised it *had* to be good to make people give up their siestas. We made a fuss at the time because we were losing trade, but after we had driven him out people went on talking, and gradually for both of us, things began to come clear until eventually they clicked into place. We've been followers of The Way ever since.

QUESTION MASTER: Is that a surprise to you, Paul?

PAUL: No, not really. Often those who are most vocal in their opposition to Christ later become his staunchest followers. I know because it happened to me. Welcome to the brotherhood of the Church. (Paul shakes hands with them.)

OPENING SENTENCE: 'I took a big risk, but then, blood is thicker than water.'

Enter PAUL'S NEPHEW

QUESTION MASTER: What was the risk that you took?

NEPHEW: My uncle was under arrest (in the Tower of Antony), not for any crime, more for protection than anything else. The Romans had rescued him from the Jews who wanted to kill him. In Jerusalem I had overheard rumours of a plot to kill him, so I went to visit my uncle and told him what I'd heard.

QUESTION MASTER: Did he seem alarmed?

NEPHEW: A bit, but not as much as many of us would. He told me to go and give details of this plot to the Roman guards. I knew that if it leaked out who had warned Paul off there would be serious trouble for me. But you can't let an innocent man walk into a death trap, especially when it's your uncle. So, I went and found the Roman chief officer.

QUESTION MASTER: What did they do?

PAUL: They whisked me off to Caesarea in the dead of night. It was a hoot really because I was surrounded by armed cavalry-men and a platoon of foot soldiers. They left us after we had reached the outskirts of the city of Jerusalem. But I'd never had such a massive escort and amongst all the soldiers' high plumed helmets I was completely hidden.

QUESTION MASTER: Wasn't it rather strange that the Romans should have taken such care to protect you?

PAUL: I owed my life to the Roman authorities on several occasions. I realise it was because I was a Roman citizen, but I feel it was all part of the divine providence which overrules these things. A man doesn't become equipped for missionary work from the moment he feels himself called of God to this service. God is ordering and arranging things from birth and even before. I don't believe that my Roman citizenship was an accident of birth. There were a lot of things like this which clicked into place when I knew myself to be 'separated unto the Gospel'.

QUESTION MASTER: Well, we're glad to have heard of this particular escape though we know it was only one amongst many.

Exit NEPHEW

OPENING SENTENCE: (AGRIPPA) 'Almost you persuaded me.'

Enter AGRIPPA *and* BERNICE

PAUL (*leaps up*): King Agrippa!

QUESTION MASTER: We are most grateful to you for coming tonight and sharing in this programme. Would you tell us, your Royal Highness, the circumstances in which you first met Paul?

BERNICE: My husband and I were visiting Porcius Festus on a state visit, and after dinner one night he began to tell us of a problem he had on his hands. A prisoner had been left over to him by his predecessor, Felix, but had committed no crime and should have been released had he not appealed to Caesar. He just didn't know what to write in his indictment and he'd look pretty stupid sending a man to Rome for no real reason. We were rather intrigued, so we asked if we might hear his defence.

AGRIPPA: Festus agreed and sent for the prisoner the next day. He was just a little chap who peered forward with the look of someone shortsighted. But, my word, when he started to talk he became like a flashing sword. His story of how he had turned from being a persecutor of the Christian Church to a pioneer missionary had the ring of truth about it. We thought it was going to be rather funny, an amusing way to spend an hour after dinner, but as I listened, I became deeply impressed, almost moved. However much you may want to laugh at a person's convictions, you cannot deny his experience, and this man, although an intellectual, did not speak simply with the gift of an orator. He spoke with the undeniable authority of personal experience.

BERNICE: We've often talked about it since. You almost had my husband joining you as a Christian, Paul.

PAUL: Well, I say to him now what I said to him then . . . 'I would that you were as I am in matters of faith.' 'Pilate saw the Truth before his eyes—yet he asked "What is Truth?" and crucified Jesus rather than face the implications of knowing the answer.'* You won't make the same mistake, will you?

AGRIPPA: We'll see. Goodbye, Paul.

* *Oblates' Rule* (C.S.M.V.)

Exit AGRIPPA *and* BERNICE

QUESTION MASTER: Paul, you were blessed with some very good and loyal friends, and only rarely in your missionary tours were you alone. We have already met Barnabas and Silas, but there were others . . .

OPENING SENTENCE: 'I'm afraid, humanly speaking, there's no cure for this one, Paul. You're going to have to live with it.'

Enter LUKE: Paul greets him with very real affection

LUKE: My dear Paul, How are you, etc.

PAUL: (Responds as naturally as possible)

QUESTION MASTER: Luke, you are a doctor and you accompanied Paul as a personal physician for some time. What stands out most clearly in your memory?

LUKE: Oh, unquestionably the shipwreck on the way to Rome.

QUESTION MASTER: Tell us about it.

LUKE: We boarded a grain ship at Myra and made across to Crete where we docked at Fairhavens. The centurion wasn't very pleased when he found that we were in a rather dead-alive hole for the winter, and the captain of the ship was even more annoyed. They both had groups of discontented men on their hands. The captain said that he thought if we hugged the coast he could make it round to Phenice where we could harbour for the winter months. You see, there was no shipping in the Mediterranean after November 11th and not much after the end of September. Well, we were running it a bit close to the dangerous period when the Euroclydon winds might spring up without warning and turn the usually calm Med. into something like a witch's cauldron. It was the centurion who had to take the decision as to whether we sailed on or not, even the captain had to defer to him. The centurion seemed to have taken a liking to Paul. He certainly respected him, so he asked Paul's opinion. Paul had been brought up in a seaport, he'd done quite a bit of sailing in his time, and he knew how treacherous the winds could be and how tricky the journey round the coast might be. He said 'No, definitely not. It's far too dangerous. You'd be much wiser to stay here at Fairhavens for the winter.' And Paul knew what he was talking about. But the captain put pressure on the centurion and in the end he agreed to try it. Well, no sooner had we got away from the shore when the inevitable happened, and we were blown right off course. Everyone was terrified and there was chaos on board. They had to undergird the boat, which is a terrific job. If we hadn't taken this precaution the damp grain would have swelled and burst the seams of the ship asunder. All excess weight had to be thrown over, and for days we just ran before the wind. Everyone feared that we would end up on the Syrtes Quicksands off the North Coast of Africa, and with no shipping coming through till the end of the winter that would have been the end of us. But all of a sudden, Paul stood up and called to everybody in a calm voice, but with a note of authority, and quietly and confidently informed them that it was going to be all right, that the boat would be lost but all lives would be saved. When he was asked how he knew, he replied that an angel of the Lord had stood by him that night and told him so. He was absolutely certain about all this. It's a moment I shall never forget because he was in complete control of the situation. Paul told everyone to get something to eat: eminently sound advice. As a doctor I know that it's the worst possible thing to feel seasick on an empty stomach, and anyway they were all suffering from shock to some extent and needed warmth.

QUESTION MASTER: And were all the lives saved?

LUKE: Oh yes, we ran on to some rocks just off Malta and the ship broke up but we all managed to get to shore, either swimming or drifting in on bits of flotsam and jetsam.

QUESTION MASTER: One thing you said at the beginning is intriguing. You spoke of something being incurable. What is this?

LUKE: Well, as a doctor I'm not allowed to disclose my patient's confidences, but let me say that Paul is a very brave man. He has come to terms with a most distressing physical complaint that gives him recurring trouble.* He still carries on with his demanding missionary work. No modern missionary would be passed as fit for service in his condition.

OPENING SENTENCE: 'The trouble is, I listened to the voice of the expert rather than the prophet.'

Enter CENTURION. Greets Paul, etc.

QUESTION MASTER: We've already heard about your shipwreck experience from Luke. But, Centurion, can you tell us something of your version? What impression did Paul make upon you?

CENTURION: A very favourable one. At first, when Paul was given into my charge I felt a great wave of pity for him. He seemed such a small, inoffensive, vulnerable little man to be making so long a journey and with such an ordeal at the end of it. But, after the first day, I realised that the small, frail-looking body housed a bundle of dynamite. He was no trouble as a prisoner, absurdly co-operative in fact, and always *most* courteous. I found myself developing a tremendous respect for him and for the faith he held too. We had several fairly long discussions, and I always found him to be very sane and sensible. There have been many, many times when I have looked back and wished with all my heart that I'd listened to Paul's advice and not to the captain. Still, I was very lucky that I lost none of my prisoners.

QUESTION MASTER: Is there anything he particularly said or did that stands out in your mind?

CENTURION: Yes, oddly enough the thing that stands out has nothing to do with the shipwreck, but the experience of the shipwreck proved that Paul was being absolutely sincere in what he said. We were on deck one day, having a discussion.

* He calls it his 'thorn in the flesh' and although he prayed for healing, the answer was not complete health but the grace to endure it.

I asked him if he wasn't sick to death of wandering from place to place, preaching, and often being persecuted for it, hounded by the Jews and jeered at by the Greeks, never knowing if he was going to have a roof over his head at night or a meal in his stomach. I've never forgotten what he said: 'I have learned in whatsoever state I am, therewith to be content.' It's stuck because I'm so often discontented myself, and I've had nothing like Paul's hardships to contend with.

QUESTION MASTER: Thank you . . . Goodbye, etc.

Exit CENTURION

QUESTION MASTER: One further contact that you had came after you had all been washed up on the shores of Malta. The inhabitants of the island were very scared of you and seemed likely to attack, but as usual you got control of the situation and managed to establish relations with the locals. There was a crisis on the island when you arrived, the Chief Man's father was very ill. . . .

OPENING SENTENCE: 'I doubt if even you will be able to do anything: he's got the bloody flux.'

Enter PUBLIUS *wh greets* PAUL

QUESTION MASTER: What on earth were you referring to just then? I fear you may have shocked some of our audience.

PUBLIUS: Oh dear! Sorry, no offence meant! It's simply the name of this particular illness which sometimes hits people in our country. It's a terribly unpleasant and usually fatal kind of dysentery, and I was nearly beside myself with worry when Paul and the others landed on our island. Rumours went round that there was a chap who had magical powers, even over snakes, and who would probably be able to cure my father. So, naturally, I sent for him. We became quite good friends during those winter months. In fact we were all very sorry when the party boarded another ship bound for Puteoli from where they were going to travel on foot to Rome. We had always hoped that Paul would be able to make a return visit.

But, alas, he was never able to come our way again. Actually, I knew the chances were remote because he was full of the idea of going on from Rome to Spain, if he got the chance. It was his great plan to use Rome as a jumping-off ground into Spain, a kind of operational base for his mission. Personally, I didn't think his health would stand another long journey and months of roughing it. But Paul himself was quite undaunted. He'd even been studying the writings of Seneca in preparation for this campaign.

QUESTION MASTER: Well, thank you very much. You've given us a most interesting piece of information that we might well not have heard otherwise.

Exit PUBLIUS

QUESTION MASTER: Publius has told us that you sailed to Puteoli and then travelled on foot to Rome. Tell us what happened when you began that last stage of the journey.

PAUL: All went smoothly in our journey and we disembarked at Puteoli and, at last, I was on Roman soil. Quite suddenly I was filled with the most appalling depression as I thought of the lonely days ahead. It was marvellous having Luke with me, but I think he felt much as I did. We hadn't gone far along the road when we saw a group of people coming towards us. They stopped and spoke to the centurion and then came to me. They were Christians from Rome, and they had come out to meet me, although it was several days' journey. I was *so* moved by the love of these brethren in Christ whom I had never met before, but who were prepared to come and welcome me like this, I wept quite unashamedly.

QUESTION MASTER: How did they know you were coming?

PAUL: I had written a letter to the Christians in Rome to prepare them for my visit, for I had met some of them during the time they were exiled under the edict of Claudius. I had come to know some at Corinth and Ephesus. They weren't able to come themselves but they sent other friends from the Church.

OPENING SENTENCE: 'I shall never forget that long trek along the Appian Way. The going was so hard, but the coming back so easy and quick in company with the great apostle.'

Enter ROMAN CHRISTIAN

QUESTION MASTER: You were one of the Christians who met him on the road then?

ROMAN CHRISTIAN: Yes, it was my privilege.

QUESTION MASTER: What happened after you reached Rome and Paul was delivered to the Roman authorities?

ROMAN CHRISTIAN: He was put under house-arrest for two years, and during that time we were free to go in and out and talk to him, though we preferred to let him talk to us. We grew in knowledge and as a body of Christians out of all recognition in those two years. As well as all his preaching and teaching, he wrote letters to some of his other churches. He had an amazing capacity for remembering people and their names, and always seemed to have an immense interest in everything about them. His spiritual children ran into hundreds, but he mentioned them all in his prayers. It was a very moving and humbling thing to see this great man seizing the opportunities to do all he could for others even in imprisonment.

QUESTION MASTER: There was one person who must have seen a great deal of you in this time of your final imprisonment, and that is the guard to whom you were chained. We're going to let this be the last word tonight.

Enter ROMAN GUARD. Greets Paul.

QUESTION MASTER: You were with Paul day and night during part of his imprisonment. You can't be with a man that long without getting to know a great deal about him. Did you, in fact, have much conversation together?

GUARD: Oh yes, we did. We often talked, and, of course, I overheard the letters he dictated. Sometimes I used to take him up on things he had written and question him. He was always very willing to explain and put them in their right setting. I used to talk quite a lot about my family, my wife and my children, and I asked Paul about his. He was peculiarly reticent about his wife. I don't think he had one. He wasn't awfully fond of women, at least that was the impression I got. He hadn't any natural children but regarded all those in the churches he had founded as his children and was enormously proud of them. I'm meeting some of them for the first time tonight, and yet I feel as though I've known them for a long time because I heard of them so much.

QUESTION MASTER: Did Paul ever try to convert you?

GUARD: Yes and no. He never missed an opportunity to talk to people about the Christian Gospel. But he never put undue pressure on me personally. He just dangled the Gospel like a dazzling jewel in front of me so that it shone and flashed in such a way that I couldn't fail to be drawn by its beauty. He never challenged me outright, but he let the Gospel loose to do its own work, and it certainly had an amazing effect in my life. Because of our own gods and way of life in Rome, I have never been able to accept the Christian God or what he claims to have done for men. I'd like to but there are too many obstacles in the way. But it has stirred up a terrible hunger and longing in my life. I've never been quite the same since: I can't find satisfaction in our household deities now. The shrines just seem to be empty, a hollow mockery of true religion. Perhaps one day . . .

I was deeply impressed by the amount of time Paul gave to prayer and meditation each day. Sometimes he was awake very early and I would find him deep in prayer . . . sometimes he even burst forth and prayed aloud. It was terrible in some ways, being in the presence of a man when he bares his soul to God.

QUESTION MASTER: Well, we hope that the divine discontent which has been stirred up in you will grow and grow until you find the answer to it. I think you know where that answer is to be found. (*To Paul*) If you had your time over again, are there things you would change? Would you adopt different tactics and methods? Have you any advice to offer to people following in your missionary footsteps?

PAUL: I don't think I'd change anything. I had to be stern when I was stern, and I'd do that again, though it cost me tears and an agony of uncertainty. I would still have appealed to Caesar: after all, it got me to Rome. If anything, I think I would have kept before me that Hymn of Love which I wrote to the Corinthian Church and would have referred to it more often and followed it as slavishly as an explorer follows a map. I think I should have pondered it far more deeply, for in *all* missionary endeavour the guiding principle and only motivation must be love. Without love all our endeavours are nothing.

INSTRUCTIONS FOR THE PREPARATION OF A PASSOVER FEAST IN A CLASSROOM

1. Plenty of background information should be given about the origins of the Passover Feast so that the enactment in the classroom is the culmination of a complete study rather than just an isolated lesson to fill in a gap at the end of term.
2. Talk to the class beforehand about the significance of the special passover food and explain the underlying meaning of each item:

   The salt water represents the tears shed by the Hebrews in slavery in Egypt.

   The bitter herbs represent the bitterness endured under Pharaoh.

   The parsley represents the hyssop used to daub the blood of the lamb on the door lintels.

   The charosheth paste (pronounced haroset) represents the mud and straw used for making the bricks in Egypt.

   The unleavened bread and roast lamb were commanded by Moses in the first passover meal and have continued to be the major items ever since.

   There are four cups of wine passed round during the meal to remind the guests of the four promises made in Exodus 6:

6, 7, but a fifth cup is placed on one side. This is reserved for Elijah lest he should arrive unexpectedly during the meal. A popular belief grew up that he would return to herald the Messiah.

3. Choose a pupil to preside as host, usually the oldest in the class, and another to ask the question in the relating, normally the youngest fulfils this function.

Give them both a chance to rehearse their parts in advance. Arrange beforehand that some children will carry the finger bowls and towels around and others pass food from one end of the horseshoe table to the other.

1. *Requirements for the Feast*

Cloths to cover the desks which should be arranged in a horseshoe shape.

Five cups for the wine, either large wine glasses or fruit bowls on stems.

Platter for the roast lamb.

Bowls for the salt water.

Finger bowls and towels (decide on a sufficient number so that the process of handwashing is not too tedious and drawn out).

Individual plates for each guest.

Separate dishes for the parsley, bitter herbs, horseradish, charosheth paste, egg and unleavened bread.

Have plenty of cloths and tissues ready in case a bowl or wine glass is upset, though obviously strict instructions should be given beforehand about the need for great care.

Give each child a copy of the order of events, or ask the children to write them down in advance. It is better *not* to have the Bibles out on the desks.

Never attempt to conduct this feast with an unruly class, or a class you have only just begun to teach. The aftermath of a disorderly Passover is unimaginable!

2. *The preparation of the food*

Roast the lamb and have it already sliced before the meal begins. A very small joint is sufficient (since this is a token meal and not meant to substitute the school lunch). It is possible that the Home Economics Department will co-operate in the loan of an oven.

The wine is best represented by Ribena, cherryade or some similar product.

Unleavened bread. Matza may be bought in many stores and supermarkets these days. If it should be unobtainable, crisp-bread or Ryvita may be used as substitutes.

Bitter herbs include parsley, horehound, endive, chicory and lettuce. These should be served separately, since not all the class will wish to sample everything.

Charosheth paste consists of a mixture of apples, pomegranates, nuts, dates and lemon juice, pulped together to represent the mud. Cinnamon sticks are stuck into it to represent the straw. Instead of pomegranates, oranges may be used. If the consistency of the mixture is too thin, it can be bound with a raw egg. If there is any paste left over at the end of the meal, it is inadvisable to let any one child eat too much of it in the clearing up. It can have adverse effects upon the stomach!

THE PASSOVER FEAST

(A suggested order of service for the Passover Feast *abbreviated to fit into one lesson of forty minutes.*)

Welcome to the guests by the host.

Host: 'Praise ye the Lord.'

Reply: 'The Lord's name be praised.'

Everyone is seated.

1. *The Cup Kiddush*

The host takes the cup and prays:

'Blessed art thou, O Lord our God, King of the Universe, who has created the fruit of the vine.'

The cup is then passed round.

2. *The First Handwashing*

The host only washes his hands three times.

3. *Parsley or Lettuce*
This is dipped in bowls of salt water and eaten.

4. *The breaking of Bread*
The host takes a piece of unleavened bread, breaks it and says:
'Blessed be thou, our Father in heaven, who givest us today the bread necessary for us.'

Only a little bread is eaten at this point. As the host breaks the rest of the bread to be handed round, he says:
'This is the bread of affliction which our forefathers ate in the land of Egypt. Whosoever is hungry, let him come and eat. Whosoever is in need, let him come and keep the Passover with us. This year we keep it here, next year in the land of Israel. This year as slaves, next year as free.'

5. *The Relating*
The youngest person present asks the host:
'What is the meaning of this Feast?'
The host replies:
'In what way is this night different from all other nights?'
The youngest person replies:
'On all other nights we eat meat boiled, stewed, roasted. On this night only roasted.
On all other nights we eat leavened or unleavened bread.
On this night only unleavened bread.
On all other nights we eat herbs of every kind.
On this night only bitter herbs.
On all other nights we dip the vegetables only once into the salt.
On this night twice.
On all other nights we have clean, fresh water.
On this night only salted water.
For this is the Passover of the Lord our God, And we will praise the Lord.'

6. *The Hallel Psalms* 113 and 114
These are then read (or sung).

7. *The Second Cup*

This is blessed and then passed round.

The host takes a sip and then hands the cup on to the person on his right.

8. *The Handwashing*

All now wash their hands in preparation for the meal.

9. *The Grace*

This is then said by the host before the meal begins:

'Blessed art thou, O Lord our God, who bringest forth fruit from the earth. Blessed art thou, O God, who hast sanctified us with thy commandment and enjoined us to eat unleavened cakes.'

The host now breaks the unleavened bread into small pieces and distributes them to the guests.

10. *Bitter Herbs*

Some of the bitter herbs are placed between two pieces of unleavened bread and then dipped in the charosheth and eaten. This is called the Sop.

11. *The Lamb*

The roasted lamb is now divided and distributed to the guests.

12. *The Handwashing*

There is a handwashing again for *all* the guests.

13. *Unleavened Bread*

The remainder of the unleavened bread is eaten.

14. *Prayer of Thanksgiving*

There is now a Prayer of Thanksgiving and blessing of the third cup:

'Blessed art thou, O Lord our God, King of the Universe, who hast created the fruit of the vine.'

15. *Hallel Psalms* 115–118 are now read (or sung).
Recommended abbreviation, Psalm 118: 1–9; 21–29.

16. *The Fourth Cup*
This is blessed and drunk.

17. *The Great Hallel*
Psalm 136, recommended abbreviation, verses 1–8 only, is said or sung.

18. *Prayers*
Two short prayers are now said by the host:

> 'All thy works shall praise thee, O Lord our God, and thy Saints, the righteous who do thy good pleasure, and all thy people, the House of Israel, with joyous song. Let them praise and bless and magnify and glorify and exalt and reverence and sanctify and scribe the Kingdom to thy name, O God, our King. For it is good to praise thee, and pleasure to sing praises to thy name, for from everlasting to everlasting, thou art God:
>
> The breath of all that lives shall praise thy name, O Lord our God. And the Spirit of all flesh shall continually glorify and exalt thy memorial, O God, our King. For from everlasting unto everlasting thou art God, and beside thee we have no King, redeemer or Saviour.'*

The feast ends with the eating up of all that remains.

* William Barclay, *The Gospel of Mark* (*Daily Study Bible Series*) (St. Andrew's Press).

5

VISUAL AIDS

There is no need to impress on anyone these days the value of visual aids in the classroom, nor what an enormous advantage it is for a teacher to have some artistic and imaginative ability, however slight! What is not, perhaps, always stressed sufficiently is the best use of visual aids as an integral part of the teaching. There is indeed a real value in letting children illustrate a story that they have heard, or an event of outstanding importance to them in their own lives (and this is especially true for the younger age ranges), but pictures are, of course, only one of a very wide variety of ways of illustrating a story or lesson.

It is important to remember that the visual aid can be just as effective as a starter to the lesson, as a follow-up. It can be the focus of interest on which the teaching is centred. This chapter discusses some of the wider possibilities of art and craft in the R.E. lesson, and the ways in which visual aids can be a real aid to understanding the content of the teaching rather than serving as jam to sweeten the pill.

Often it is assumed that the need for visual aids with older age-groups can be adequately met by introducing illustrative material such as the occasional films, maps, photographs, reproductions of religious art and wall charts, whereas the need to express their conceptual thinking in visual forms is as real for the pupil in the secondary as in the primary school. Care is needed to find the best media.

One group of sixth form girls was asked by their Art Mistress to produce a painting that represented the combined efforts of the group. They chose the Resurrection of Christ as their subject and read and re-read a dozen times the stories of the Crucifixion and

Resurrection. They argued, discussed, questioned and then painted. The result was startling and very moving, and all the more significant since the group included a Jewess and several sincere agnostics as well as those of orthodox Christian belief.

Another group displayed a frieze on the subject of Creation running from one end to the other of an extremely long corridor. Many of the subjects chosen for painting, paper sculpture, carving and pottery by senior pupils are religious. They are driven by the impulse which has governed all artists down through the ages, the impulse to express one's deepest feelings about life, its problems and relationships in visible form.

The fact that this kind of activity is time-consuming perhaps accounts for the more conservative methods still used by some R.E. teachers, who find it difficult to escape the feeling that this is rather a waste of valuable teaching time. This feeling is very understandable when one bears in mind the strictly limited time given to R.E. in most time tables. In secondary school general courses it may be one lesson a week, at most two.

There are additional practical difficulties in such work since many schools are unable to allot a special room to R.E. Therefore, all sorts of extra arrangements have to be made for working with paint, paste, glue, wood, mosaics, plaster, plasticine, etc., in an ordinary classroom: paper on the desks, overalls on the children, strict precautionary measures where jars of water or glue are being used, and such thorough clearing up afterwards that the cleaner would never guess what had been going on, let alone be given grounds for complaint. With careful planning and organisation, however, these practical difficulties may be overcome, and though entailing far more work for the teacher, it is immensely worthwhile in the long run.

Perhaps the greatest difficulty is not at the practical, organisational level, but in seeing how this can truly be called education and lead to a better understanding of a particular biblical topic. Certainly one must be able to justify the amount of time spent in working on a practical project and see from the beginning its possibilities and potential teaching value. In seeing clearly the value of such projects there is a danger that they may become too important and too time-consuming. Furthermore, not all classes will welcome this kind of practical work as they do so much of it in other subjects. It would be advisable to check on this before beginning a project with any particular class. If it *is* done, it must be done very well indeed or it will rightly draw criticism from other departments that are trying to encourage high standards in their fields.

There are a number of most helpful books to suggest how to make models and charts (some of which are mentioned in the bibliography), but the link-up between the visual and the verbal is not always made explicit. In this chapter, a number of suggestions are made not only about various media but also about teaching material that can be based upon the visual aid.

Model-making

The following ideas for model-making are intended to show how the model may be the means of illustrating and introducing biblical material. Dozens of other ideas may be worked out on the same principle. In all cases it is advisable to make the models as large as possible.

PALESTINIAN HOME

A model of a simple village home could become the focal point for introducing the following material:

1. *The friend who came at midnight to ask for bread* (Luke 11: 5–8) With the aid of a model showing the two floor levels in a village home (the platform on which the family slept, and the floor level where the animals bedded down), it will be seen that to get up and go to the door at that hour of night would cause pandemonium in the house. The family and animals alike would be disturbed and wakened from their deep sleep. Therefore the refusal of the householder was quite reasonable, and yet the persistent knocking of his needy friend was commendable and wholly understandable in the light of Jewish rules of hospitality. To have no bread to set before a

visitor was the height of discourtesy, and yet many housewives baked only enough bread for one day's needs, not allowing for unexpected guests (a comment on the average standard of living?).

2. *The Lost Coin* (Luke 15: 8–9)
The model could include some of the goods and chattels of the household showing how well-nigh impossible it would be to find one small coin amongst all the straw of the animals, and the cooking utensils and bedding of the family.

3. *Lights*
(a) under bushels. Model lamps would illustrate why (for safety's sake) they needed to be placed under bushels if the family was leaving the house for a while after 'lighting-up' time, and why they needed to be placed
(b) on lampstands while the family were in, so that they would give light to all that are in the house (Matthew 5: 15).
(Ref.: A. C. Bouquet's *Everyday Life in New Testament Times*, p. 46.)

4. *Laying up treasure* (Matthew 6: 19–21)
Through the model and a discussion on the fabric of Palestinian homes, the meaning of Jesus's teaching on 'not laying up treasure on earth' would become clear. It would be seen:
(a) how easy it would be for thieves to 'break through and steal' when all they would need to do would be to scrape a hole through the mud wall and reach into the house for the money stored there.
(b) how often the household granary could become infested with rats, maggots or weevils that would slowly eat away the food supply which was a real form of wealth. (N.B. 'rust', here means that which eats away.)
(c) how, very probably, clothes kept in storage chests would get the moth in them and the fine linen (another investment of wealth) would be ruined.
The central courtyard in the larger type of house would illustrate:

5. *The healing of the paralytic borne of four* (Mark 2: 1–12)
It would show the outer staircase and the kind of flat roof which was so easy to break through.

6. *Eating with publicans and sinners*
The way in which Jesus was publicly observed whilst feasting with the outcasts of society (Mark 2: 15–17; Luke 5: 27–32).

The flat roof would serve to illustrate the stories of:

7. *Elisha and the Shunemite woman*
Include in the model the extra room sometimes built on the roof (2 Kings 4: 10).

8. *Peter's vision*
On the rooftop at Joppa (Acts 10: 9–33).

9. *Jesus' warnings about the coming destruction of Jerusalem*
People would have to jump from rooftop to rooftop (Matthew 24: 17; Mark 13: 15).
(Ref.: A. C. Bouquet's *Everyday Life in New Testament Times*, pp. 29–31.)

A SYNAGOGUE

Link the model-making with a visit to a local synagogue (if possible) and show photos of ancient synagogues (e.g. *Everyday Life in New Testament Times*, p. 217), and a film or filmstrip of synagogue worship in Palestine.

The model itself will be of the greatest teaching value if it is large enough to include an ark containing miniature scrolls and covered by velvet curtains. The making of the scrolls and the writing out of Hebrew texts could be the work of one small group, while stitching and embroidering the curtains could be the work of another group. Other pupils could be engaged in making the furniture of the synagogue: the pews, pulpit, women's gallery, lamps, etc. Another group could make a number of figures out of pipe cleaners or plasticine and dress them showing the prayer shawl (tallith) and phylacteries.

The following material could be introduced as the work on the model progresses:

(i) The synagogue was the village school, as well as the centre of worship, and it would have been here that Jesus would have received his formal education.

(ii) All Jews attended the synagogue on the Sabbath. Jesus himself made it his custom (Luke 4: 16).

Even though the teaching was often uninspiring they continued faithfully in this practice. When Jesus was asked to speak it was a service with a difference for 'he taught them as one that had authority, and not as the scribes' (Mark 1: 22). Give some description of scribal methods of preaching. It was customary to invite visiting rabbis and itinerant preachers to speak in the synagogue (Luke 4: 16–21).

(iii) Give some outline of the order of worship in a synagogue service and show how it has changed very little over the centuries. Make *sure* the pupils fully understand the difference between synagogue worship and Temple ritual.

(iv) Show how the pattern of synagogue worship evolved from the Exile onwards: the need during the Exile to replace the sacrifices of the Temple with the Law as the focal point of worship.

Show how the concentration on the Law and its implications, though very good in the first place, had led to ridiculous excesses and an enormous accretion of pettifogging little rules gathered together in the Mishnah (the Scribal law). Hence Jesus condemned the Scribes and Pharisees for their legalistic attitude and hardness of heart (Matthew 23) and introduced a new and simplified commandment (Matthew 22: 36–40).

With seniors this could lead to a study of the history of the origins of the Scribes and Pharisees to see how the situation, as Jesus found it, had developed.

(v) The figures wearing phylacteries would help to illuminate the words of Jesus in Matthew 23: 5.

(vi) Show through the women's gallery, the confusion that would have resulted from women calling out to their husbands down in the body of the synagogue, hence St. Paul's misunderstood words about 'women keeping silence in church', i.e. not calling out and interrupting with questions that ought properly to be asked and answered at home (1 Corinthians 14: 34).

THE TEMPLE

(Useful ground plan on p. 196 of *Everyday Life in New Testament Times.*)

Most of the relevant teaching material for this model will be found in the theme 'The Stones Cry Out' in Chapter 1, page 39.

Although a large model would take up a great deal of space if all the courts were included, it is well worth attempting it so that the details (the sea of brass, the altar of sacrifice, etc.) may be shown. The colonnades may be made out of old Smartie tubes and the rest of the Temple area scaled accordingly. Full instructions for the making of the Temple are found in *Models for the Scripture Lesson* by Marjorie Barwell.

The making of costumes

PALESTINIAN CLOTHES

Ideally two sets of clothes should be made, for men and women, out of old sheets, thin blankets, bedspreads, etc. Draw out the patterns and describe each article of clothing leaving the group to do the stitching. (If old sheets are torn up and used, it may be possible to enlist the help of the Art Department, and dye the material with vegetable dyes.) Smaller children who cannot manage anything so ambitious could dress dolls or pipe cleaner figures in Palestinian garments.

If it is not possible to make a full-sized set of clothes with older pupils, it is quite effective to draw them in the exercise books or on wall charts using collage work for the headgear, sandals, belt, etc.

The following garments should be made:

1. *The Outer Cloak* (Himation)

This will illustrate:

(i) Matthew 5: 40: 'Whosoever takes away thy tunic, let him have thy cloak also.' Show how the coat becomes a blanket at night and could not legally be taken from a man since the law protected a man from the loss of his bedding. (N.B. the teaching of Jesus that his followers were not to stand by their rights.)

(ii) When the disciples were sent out on a mission (Matthew 10: 9–10) they were expected to exercise great faith. They were instructed not to be over-cautious about their material needs during the mission, and amongst other things were not to take two coats

(iii) The coat was discarded during manual work. When Jesus warned people of the days of destruction in Jerusalem, he advised men 'in that hour' not to stop even to pick up their coats from the edge of the fields, but to flee for their lives (Mark 13: 16; Matthew 24: 18).

(iv) These were the garments which the excited crowds 'spread in the way' as Jesus entered Jerusalem on a donkey (Mark 11: 8).

(v) It was the outer cloak that Paul particularly needed in prison (presumably for warmth during the day and bedding at night) and asked John Mark to bring to him (2 Timothy 4: 13).

2. *The Tunic* (Chiton)

This long flowing garment was somewhat cumbersome. Describe how these tunics were 'gathered up' and tucked into the belt when men needed to be unimpeded for action. It was referred to as 'girding up the loins' and became a figure for energetic action, e.g.:

(i) 'He looseth the bond of kings, and girdeth their loins with a girdle' (Job 12: 18).

(ii) Simon Peter 'girt his fisher's coat unto him' (John 21: 7).

(iii) Peter's escape from prison (Acts 12: 8).

This is the garment which Joseph was given by his father which caused such jealousy (Genesis 27).

The ordinary tunic was made in at least three ways:

(i) It might consist of two similar pieces of woollen or linen cloth cut from a large web which were sewed together along the sides and top.

(ii) The material for a single tunic might be woven on the loom, and afterwards put together without cutting, in the manner of the Egyptian tunics.

(iii) As we know from the description of the *Chiton* worn by our

Lord at the time of his passion (John 19: 23) and from other sources, a third variety was woven 'without seam' on a special loom and required no further adjustment. (*Hastings' Dictionary of the Bible*, p. 197.)

3. *The Belt* (or girdle)

It varied in material from 'a simple rope to the rich and elaborate waist-belt of the priests, and the "golden girdles" of Rev. 1: 13; 15: 6'. (*Hastings' Dictionary of the Bible.*)

Frequently the belt was a wide piece of material folded over to form pockets in which dried fruit, nuts, cheese and money were kept. This too was referred to in Jesus's instructions for missions to his disciples (Matthew 10: 9–10). They were not to fill their wallets with emergency rations but were to have faith that hospitality would be offered them.

The unfortunate victim who was attacked and robbed in the story of 'The Good Samaritan' would probably have been carrying all his money in his belt, which he would have lost when beaten up and 'stripped of his raiment' (Luke 10: 30).

The belt also served as a sword-belt (2 Samuel 20: 8) and through it the writer would stick his inkhorn (Ezekiel 9: 3, 11).

4. *The Sandals*

Model the different varieties of sandal. Sandals are also mentioned:

(i) In Jesus's instructions to his disciples(Mark 6: 9; Matthew 10: 10; Luke 10: 4).

(ii) In Acts 12: 8 when Peter escaped from prison.

(iii) When Paul and Barnabas left Antioch in Pisidia and symbolically abandoned the city by shaking the dust from their shoes on the city boundaries (Acts 13: 51).

It was considered a menial task to remove someone's sandals. In the schools it fell to the most insignificant pupil (the youngest boy) to remove the sandals of the rabbi. John the Baptist claimed that the 'one who was to come' would be so great that he, John, would be unworthy so much as to unloose the latchet of his shoes (Mark 1: 7).

One of the evidences of the caring of the father in the story of the

Prodigal Son was that he not only provided the best robe, and a ring for his son's finger, but shoes for his feet (Luke 15: 22).

5. *The Headdress*

In New Testament times, the headdress for men was a rectangular piece of cloth placed over the head and held in place by a band. For the women the veil was much longer of course. In Old Testament times a sort of turban had been worn by both sexes and is referred to variously in the A.V. as hood, mitre and royal diadem.

Heads were *always* covered for worship, of course, but the main need for headgear was for protection from the sun, and for wiping away perspiration. This was the napkin of John 11: 44; 20: 7.

Women throughout the East kept their heads covered in public and were thought to be of dubious character if they did not. Hence Paul's advice to the Corinthian Christian women that although they now lived under grace and not under law, it would be wise to keep their heads covered when praying and prophesying lest non-Christians should grossly misunderstand their actions (1 Corinthians 11: 5).

Aids for background study

FURTHER MODEL-MAKING

For a background study of life in Bible times it may be helpful to make further models of:

1. *Fishing boats*

Show the kind of boat in which Jesus travelled (even sleeping through a storm, Mark 4: 36) and from which he preached (Matthew 13: 2).

2. *Different kinds of fishing nets*

These show:

(a) how the disciples would spend whole nights fishing out on the lake (John 21: 3–4).

(b) how they would have fished from the lakeside (casting their nets).

(c) how the nets would need regular mending, a job the fishermen would do during the daytime, sitting at the lakeside (Mark 1: 19).

3. *A Sheepfold*
This illustrates Jesus's teaching about the Good Shepherd (John 10: 1–18), the Lost Sheep (Luke 15: 3–7) and even his reference to 'other sheep which are not of this fold' in John 10.
(Ref.: H. V. Morton's *In the Steps of the Master*.)

4. *A Potter's Wheel and Kiln*
As illustrative material for a study of Palestinian trades and occupations and also for Jeremiah's teaching (Jeremiah 18: 2, 3). Link this work with some study of what is known of Palestinian pottery from Petrie's *Tell el Hesy*; Bliss's *Mound of Many Cities*; and *Excavations in Palestine* by Bliss, Macalister and Wünsch.
(Cf. *Everyday Life in New Testament Times*, pp. 48–50).

5. *A Garden Tomb*
Study photographs of typical tombs (e.g. *Everyday Life in New Testament Times*, p. 208) and also reconstructions of the kind of tomb in which the body of Jesus would have been laid. If possible have photographs of the gardens in Jerusalem now believed to be possible sites of the original tomb.

Possibly the cheapest material for making a model of such a tomb is plaster of paris which can be applied thickly to a framework of wire meshing.

6. *A Carpenter's Shop*
Show all the probable tools used, and some of the finished products, e.g. stools, tables, cupboards, ploughs, yokes.
(cf: *Everyday Life in New Testament Times*, pp. 51–52.)

7. *A Vineyard*
Include the watch tower, hedge, wine press, etc. Link this with:

Isaiah (Isaiah 5: 1–7). The Parable of the Wicked Husbandmen (Matthew 21: 33–45).

8. *Mediterranean Sailing Ships*

These illustrate travel by sea in the first century, especially the travels of St. Paul (ref: Sir William Ramsay). A. C. Bouquet, *Everyday Life in New Testament Times.* Bernard Youngman's *Spreading the Gospel.* R. H. Horton's *Stories of the Early Church 4.*

Include the kind of tackle that would have been used to undergird a grain ship, also a long boat, sails and masts. To complete the model, make a quayside to show the business of ports at that time as now.

9. *An Inn*

Showing the kind of accommodation that was refused to Joseph and Mary and provided for the robbed man in the story of the Good Samaritan.

MATERIAL IN DISPLAY FORM

Besides models, much useful information may be gained from presenting material in display form, either by:

(a) drawing and painting on wall charts with descriptive notes
(b) making objects in balsa wood or card and sticking them on to wall charts with notes
(c) making objects in clay, plasticine, wood, plaster, etc., and arranging them on a display tray or table, with each item clearly labelled as in a museum.

The following ideas may be presented in one form of display or another:

(i) Palestinian household utensils (clay, plasticine, wood or card).
(ii) Surgical and dental instruments of the first century A.D. (aluminium foil, tin, wire, wood).
(iii) Musical instruments of the Bible (bamboo cane, balsa wood, wire, string, gut).
(iv) Cosmetic and toilet articles in biblical times (card, clay, tin foil, pins, matchboxes, beads, balsa wood, wire, etc.)

(v) Palestinian farming implements and farming methods (wood, balsa wood, cane, raffia).
(vi) Ancient writing techniques (clay or plasticine made into tablets, wedge-shaped stick prints made out of pieces of chalk, papyrus reeds).
(vii) Roman, Greek and Jewish coinage (plasticine, papier mâché, cardboard, silver and gold paper).
(viii) Metallurgical instruments of the first century A.D. (tin foil, wire, string, balsa wood, card).

The illustration of ideas

So far the models and displays suggested have been to illustrate facts, but visual aids are also helpful in the realm of ideas. Here one can be even more imaginative and adventurous.

I remember the class that produced their visual representation of the Vision and Call of Isaiah with an interior scene of the Sanctuary of the Temple. From the altar of incense there rose a coil of grey (tissue paper) smoke ascending to the ceiling and affixed thereto with a drawing pin, looking every bit like 'the train that filled the Temple'. Behind the altar was the raised Holy of Holies 'high and lifted up' obscured simply by a muslin veil to represent the fact that in his vision Isaiah 'saw' through the veil to the throne of God, the mercy seat covering the ark. The group had made an ark with a gold leaf covering and seraphim in paper sculpture each with six muslin wings hovered over the ark spanning the Holy of Holies from wall to wall. From behind the ark there shone a light from a concealed torch bulb representing the Shekinah glory and giving the full 3D effect. In the foreground of the model were figures in paper sculpture of priests moving about their duties. The entrance to the Sanctuary was flanked by the two pillars (Joachim and Boaz) and the doorposts which moved with the vibration of the priests' singing and against which the young Isaiah was leaning. The whole thing was beautifully done and very effective.

Another group attempted to interpret the vision in ceramics, and although this was a difficult medium, they really managed to capture something of the glory of the Lord and wonder of the whole experience for Isaiah.

There was the class that illustrated the heartache of Hosea by making composite pictures. Using cuttings from magazines, they showed what appeared at first to be a jumble of faces and figures, but on closer inspection revealed a careful choice of photos showing despair, suffering, shame and bewilderment: faces of men worried, heartbroken, searching and hunting; faces of children bewildered and abandoned (and one does not have to look far for such photos these days); faces of women who have enjoyed a so-called 'good time' only to be followed by the aftermath of wretchedness and shame. The arrangement of these pictures was nothing like as kaleidoscopic as a casual glance would suggest. Rather there was a deliberate attempt to draw the eye inward through the varying degrees of misery to the crux of the story, a brokenhearted love that overflowed with forgiveness.

A similar technique can be used for illustrating the teaching of Amos. Bold headlines of Amos's condemnations in modern journalistic style, may be illustrated by modern day pictures and newspaper cuttings of cheating and swindling, false weights and measures, bribery and corruption, injustice where there should be justice, gross inequality between the poor (homeless and starving) and the rich (overfed and sporting their town houses and country houses), land-grabbing and servitude amounting to slavery, false religion (i.e. religious practices that are totally divorced from everyday life). All of this may be seen to be the twentieth-century dilemma to which Amos has something very relevant to say. Presented in this visual way it can make a great impact.

It is sometimes possible to present a series of ideas in the form of a set of stained-glass windows, by using thick card and coloured cellophane paper. A modern version of the seven deadly sins, the cardinal virtues, or the fruits of the Spirit may be presented in this way. Or scenes from the life of a saint, or a series of scenes from the lives of a number of saints (ancient and modern) make good subjects. Or again, a series of windows illustrating scenes in the life of Jesus, or the parables of Jesus would be more suitable for the younger age-groups.

In the secondary school course, most syllabuses include a little elementary biblical criticism in the first two years, usually under the title of the Bible Library. Here again a visual aid can be of great help and increase the interest and understanding of a class. Often the Bible Library is illustrated in textbooks in the form of a row of books on a bookshelf. I found it even more interesting actually to make book ends, and then a series of books out of empty cereal packets. These were covered with different coloured papers and the back of each book not only bore the title (e.g. Law, Poetry, History, Romance, Prophecy, etc.) but also opened outwards to reveal, inside the empty carton, a scroll. On each scroll was written a parable, or a psalm, or a short historical account to illustrate the diversity of material to be found in the Bible.

Where it was not possible to make the large scale model of the library, I found pupils enjoyed drawing the row of books in their exercise books, and then sticking a series of backs on to the drawing (on the left-hand side of the 'back' only) so that they flapped open to reveal written inside a short text illustrating the different kinds of material.

Whilst it may take a little while to make the library, it is possible to divide a class into groups and work on one section each, and the real value is that it sends them hunting through the parables, the psalms, the adventure stories, etc., to select their choice for the scroll. Probably it entails more actual reading of the Bible than any one other part of the first and second year syllabus.

With the upper age ranges in a secondary school, Religious Education usually takes the form of discussion groups where moral, social and religious issues are thrashed out. The sixth form general group is often the hardest place of all to relate the biblical message to discussions, not because the relevance is not clear, but because there is often considerable resistance on the part of the pupils. Quite naturally and rightly they want to know of the claims made by other religions on issues such as life after death, creation, worship and ethics. They do not necessarily accept the Bible as authoritative and relevant and they want to cast their net more widely amongst the varying creeds and philosophies. Very often, in this stage of not knowing what to believe or why, when they are honest agnostics, they claim to be hardened atheists with 'no time for all that religious stuff'. However, under the apparent hostility or indifference, there is often a real search going on, and whilst this could not be easily articulated in words, it shows through in other creative ways. With perhaps one short period a week for sixth form general groups, there is not sufficient time to experiment in this more fully, but occasionally a student will produce a work of art in his own time, simply from the sheer need to express some inner struggle of thought. Or, if the student takes Art, it is interesting to see that sometimes the recent discussions in R.E. are reflected in abstract paintings. Subjects such as birth, death and conflict are quite common. I remember a Congolese student (before Independence and the riots and bloodshed that followed) presenting an abstract painting on the theme of war. It was one of the most powerful paintings I have ever seen, and I marvelled that it had come from a young man who had absolutely no personal experience of war; the most he would have known at first hand would have been a tribal feud. The paintings displayed by the Art Departments in colleges and universities are constant reminders of the depth and trends of thought going on amongst students and of the need of many to express them in visual ways. There was the beautifully carved maquette representing Justice done by a sixth form boy, and the different attempts to present the Virgin and Child by some sixth form girls in sculpture classes. Some of the results were moving in their simplicity and in the very way that great love and tenderness were starkly exposed.

It is because there is great need for thinking young people to express themselves in the outward and visible, that, as with Drama and Dance, there is a real place for teamwork with the Art and Craft Department. Through discussions and study in the R.E. lessons thoughts and questions are stirred to life that begin to batter inside the student for release. That release may come through the written word, or through music, but it may equally well come through Art, and it is the contribution of the Art Department to encourage those skills which will make possible the expression of awakening thoughts. The integrated studies now time tabled for many sixth forms will make this a growing possibility for an increasing number of young people.

VISUAL AIDS IN THE SCHOOL ASSEMBLY

Some of these visual aids may be used to help in the school assembly. The stained-glass windows, if large enough, could be fixed to the windows of the school hall where they would show up very clearly against the light. Alternatively, if a study of the lives of saints, church leaders, social reformers, etc., is being carried out, large paintings of life-sized figures hung on the walls are very effective. Such a series could perhaps be timed to coincide with All Souls' and All Saints' Day.

Sometimes it is possible to arrange display units around the hall or at the back of it, so that pupils can study the exhibits as they leave the hall. One group of first-year pupils in a secondary school was asked to conduct an assembly and chose as its theme 'Hands'. They made a large scale plaster model of Durer's wood carving *The Praying Hands* and told the story behind it. They showed on a screen a photograph of Rodin's sculpture of hands, *Le Cathédrale*, and told the story of the way in which Auguste Rodin's sister had worked to earn extra money to support her brother as he trained as an artist. They discussed some of the miracles of craftsmanship and musicianship wrought by man's greatest instruments, his hands, and one girl had written a poem which was read as a prayer. At the back of the hall and along the corridor leading to it, they displayed pictures painted without hands by artists of the Mouth and Foot Association. This continued the interest after the actual assembly was over.

Senior pupils may well be able to set up display units and exhibitions showing something of the work done by such organisations as Shelter, Oxfam, Save the Children Fund, etc., making the theme of the assembly, 'Caring for Others' and pin-pointing one or two stories of real need and loneliness to show just how important the contribution of voluntary social services is. They may also find it helpful to show some of the findings and statistics of a social survey of the area in which the school is situated in a series of flow diagrams and charts. Many of the problems of the world and local community about which teenagers feel so strongly make suitable themes for assemblies and will produce a far greater impact with the use of really good visual aids.

The seasons of the Church's year are obvious and proper themes for assemblies and in seeking new ideas we must not discard all that is old and traditional. Nativity scenes and Easter gardens are still well loved and may be produced in papier mâché or paper sculpture, or, where possible, figures may be modelled in clay and baked in the kiln. It would be good to see more attempts in painting or collage work to celebrate Ascensiontide and Whitsun.

Many churches no longer collect food products at harvest time since the the greatest needs are not necessarily in our own communities but overseas. Instead, money is raised to buy farming or medical equipment to send to underdeveloped countries. In many city schools this is a more sensible idea and exciting schemes are often carried out. Posters showing conditions in these countries act as an incentive to giving, and since young people like to see what is happening with their money and the end product of their efforts, rather than hear simply that a cheque has been sent off, it is a good idea to have the project on display and centre the thoughts of the assembly on it with, possibly, an expert explaining how the equipment is to be used. Schools have collected for such varied items as tape recorders, film projectors, blood transfusion units, bush hogs, new roofs for chapels or schools, water pumps, large apparatus for P.E. and various spare parts for machinery, cars or land-rovers. Obviously some of these could not be introduced into a school hall, nor is it possible to demonstrate them all in an assembly. A school might, for instance, decide to raise money for a scholarship to help train a teacher, agriculturalist or journalist in the Third World. It would not be particularly easy to support this scheme with any kind of visual aid other than posters or by showing transparencies of the particular countries involved. They may decide to send money to increase the livestock in a certain area, and again the actual purchase could not be displayed, though where schools have raised money to train guide dogs for the blind, the Guide Dogs for the Blind Association continues the interest by allowing the school to choose the name of the dog. Then when training is completed a framed photo is sent as a memento. Though it would be delightful to have the dog at the school for a morning, this practice is not encouraged by the Association. Sometimes, however, local blind people who already have dogs are prepared to come and talk about the ways in which they depend upon them. Many schools in Africa and Asia are in desperate need of books, particularly mission schools that rely to a great extent on voluntary gifts. A collection of books, ranging over a wide number of interests, would be a better idea for a harvest thanksgiving than the collection of fruit, vegetables and dairy produce. It is possible, of course, to make a collection of non-perishable foods, and there are still many countries where there is a crying need for essentials such as dried milk. If schools particularly want to make their harvest contribution in the form of foodstuffs, the Save the Children Fund will always advise on what is most needed at the time.

6
BEYOND THE SCHOOL

One of the observations which Dr. Goldman makes in *Religious Thinking from Childhood to Adolescence** is that 'about the time when more abstract thinking becomes possible, and so more religious insights can be seen, many adolescents appear to lose interest in religion, or develop more negative attitudes to religion. This appears to be less of a problem with brighter and girl pupils'.

Many R.E. teachers sense the waning interest in the subject in the third or fourth year of the secondary school (perhaps even sooner) and greatly regret this loss of interest at the very age when insights should be deepening and something really valuable might be achieved. It seems to indicate two things. Firstly, much solid work must be done in the years prior to the 'falling off' period. Stress has very rightly been laid upon introducing topics that are suited to the age and experience of the child, and selecting biblical material that will enable him to build up adequate concepts of God, but we need always to be certain that our pupils are being stretched enough. Sometimes they are capable of far deeper insights than we imagine. For instance, in one school an experiment was carried out amongst children of seven to nine years. They were given a selection of hymn books, some of which were used in the school, and some in Sunday School and junior churches, and were asked to pick out their favourites. In almost every case, the hymns chosen were those that were deeply doctrinal, speaking of the great truths of the Christian faith, not necessarily those especially written for children of their age-group.

* Dr. Goldman, *Religious Thinking from Childhood to Adolescence* (p. 21).

Of course, the appeal of the tune may have influenced some choices, but this could not possibly have accounted for every case.

When children enter the secondary school, they are often very excited by the many new subjects they are beginning; their horizons are being broadened, and their minds stretched in numerous ways. It is essential that this should happen in R.E. too, and that they do not feel that here they are repeating junior school work. The head of the R.E. Department may have a very difficult decision to make in putting in time table requests to the Head. He knows that the fourth- and fifth-year classes are hard going, and usually more problematic in terms of discipline. He is tempted, therefore, to give the younger age-groups to the junior and less experienced members of the department since these are far less 'anti' the subject and therefore easier to manage. Such a solution may not always be the right one. The first two years in the secondary school are very important, for sometimes the major part of the R.E. teaching is done in the primary school and during these two years. It is in this period that foundations are laid, a healthy respect for the subject formed, and right attitudes to life encouraged. M.V.C. Jeffreys may be right in certain respects when he says '. . . education is a matter of attitudes rather than information'.*

Secondly, if the foundations have been securely laid and the right attitudes encouraged, then the overt lack of interest may not be as disastrous as it at first seems. There will never be room for complacency over this, of course, and a dearth of interest in the thirteen- to fifteen-year age-group will be a constant headache to the R.E. teacher, but it would be wrong to become unduly distressed by it. Unless a pupil has close connections with a church, and/or a strong Christian influence from home, he is unlikely to show enthusiasm openly even though he may well be thinking deeply in private. Sometimes a parents' evening will bring wholly unexpected and pleasant surprises when one learns from parents that a pupil, who has never appeared to be particularly interested in the subject, frequently discusses R.E. lessons at home and thoroughly enjoys

* M. V. C. Jeffreys, *Religion and Morality* (R.E.P.), p. 100.

the work that is being done. However, there are many pupils at this stage who are 'lying fallow' and do not particularly want to face up to moral and theological problems. This reluctance may be variously related to the rate of physical growth, intellectual ability, home environment, quality of previous R.E. teaching, etc. These are the pupils who may well benefit most from the practical outworking of some of the attitudes encouraged in earlier R.E. lessons (e.g. friendship, caring for others, loving service that wants only to give, etc.) through social service activities beyond the school.

In my own experience, it has been interesting to note over the years, how the pupils who volunteered most readily to help in social service work and gave unstintingly of their time and energy, were often those who were very obviously 'lying fallow' as far as R.E. lessons were concerned. It cannot, of course, be held that their enthusiasm and eagerness to serve were necessarily the outcome of earlier R.E. teaching, nor that eventually they came back to study more closely the claims of the Christian faith and the teaching of Jesus. But sometimes one has proof that this does happen. From their practical work 'in the field' pupils sometimes come back to look with different eyes and a new respect at Jesus's insistence upon the infinite worth and importance of each individual; at his apparently topsy-turvy values that so upset the good, religious folk of his day; at his preference for the outcasts and sinners of society rather than the (self) righteous; at his clear teaching that the sins of the mind are as culpable as the sins of the body, that motive and action must both come under the same condemnation, that in his Kingdom 'the creed and the colour and the name don't matter'.

If this kind of teaching, with especial emphasis upon the selfless love of Jesus demonstrated supremely in the Cross, has been taught thoroughly and vividly in the earlier years of the secondary school and in the primary school, then undoubtedly it will have an influence on some, if not all, of the pupils. This will be more pronounced if they see it made real in the lives and actions of those who profess to believe that it is part of the truth of God. It is not that certain views have 'rubbed off', that would simply be a form of brain washing. It is much more that they have been educated in value judgements.

The pupils' desire to help and comfort the poor and lonely, the real heartache they feel for the children of broken marriages living *in transit* in Corporation-run homes waiting for foster parents to be found, their willingness to give up valuable time to play with the handicapped children, may be due to the fact that they are of sympathetic natures and show an unusual gratitude for their own good fortune and health, but I suspect that much of the religious education they have received has imperceptibly become part of their own thinking, although they may be as unware of the source of their compassion as they are of the origin of their taste for Debussy.

Once more it must be stressed that Christians cannot claim a monopoly where 'good works' are concerned. Christian faith must express itself in good works (for faith without works is dead) and a religion that speaks of loving God without loving one's neighbour is worthless. But not all good works are the direct result of Christian faith, and we cannot but recognise honestly before our pupils that humanists have contributed greatly to the alleviation of various forms of suffering and human misery. However, since the humanist is also made in the image of God, the Christian may be able to explain more clearly than the humanist himself why he is loving and compassionate.

Almost every secondary school, and even some primary schools have a social service programme these days. Sometimes the social service work is done during school hours, but mostly it is service rendered in the pupils' and staff's own free time. In the majority of schools the social service programme seems to be directed by the R.E. Department, but there are some schools where this is a post of responsibility in itself. As has already been suggested earlier in the chapter, it is of immense educational value to the R.E. Department to have this work under its umbrella, even though it makes for a great deal of hard work. It is especially helpful for the R.E. teacher to have a normal working relationship with those pupils who loathe R.E. as a subject and may even have opted out of lessons. It provides him with a continued contact that would otherwise be impossible, and leaves a way open for a come-back if the pupil should ever have a change of heart where this area of experience is concerned.

Social service

The following are possible ideas, many of them already in practice in schools, for social work in the local community. Comments and warnings are given where applicable.

OLD PEOPLE

1. *Visiting*

A list of elderly people and shut-ins in the local community can be obtained from the local welfare officer or the Meals on Wheels service. It is best for pupils to go visiting in pairs. Stress should be laid on the fact that the visits should be fairly short but they *must* be regular since the old people look forward to them. There must be no casual attitude that might bring disappointment. Any cases of acute need should be reported back to a member of staff, as also any pressure for money or undue demands for heavy manual work in the house or garden. Pupils sometimes need protection when the purpose of their visits is not entirely understood.

The list of elderly people should be revised every term, so that Christmas and Harvest gifts, etc., do not get sent to the deceased, causing distress both to relatives and the pupil visitors.

It is advisable to work in conjunction with the local clergy as well as the welfare officer to avoid unnecessary duplication of visitors when other lonely folk are left out.

2. *Gifts*

Parcels of groceries at Christmas are usually very welcome but where this might cause offence, gifts such as calendars, writing materials and handkerchieves show the old people that they are not forgotten. It is as well to give uniform gifts since they may get together and compare notes. Sometimes a packet of Christmas cards (that they themselves can then send out) is the most acceptable gift at that season.

Depending upon the number of old people cared for by the school and the state of the social service funds, it might be possible to recognise each old person's birthday with a card and/or gift. Sometimes pupils organise this themselves. They grow so fond of the old person they visit, that without any suggestion from an adult, they buy a card and present out of their own pocket money. Two girls were asked to visit an elderly person with a Christmas parcel, and when they arrived and found her lying in a very small, squalid room where the air was foul and everything was depressingly dirty, they went straight out and bought pot plants to brighten up the room, and fresh flowers to sweeten it. It was a season when flowers were at their dearest yet they refused all offers to be reimbursed from the social service funds.

Where schools have ground that can be cultivated, it may be possible to grow flowers and vegetables for distribution to the old people who cannot afford to buy them for themselves. If there is no available gardening space in the school grounds, pupils may be encouraged to do a spot of cultivating at home.

3. *Entertainment*

This may include:

Christmas parties with carol concerts.

Carol singing in groups at the private homes of elderly people and especially in Old People's Homes.

Summer garden parties with dancing and P.E. displays, musical items and community singing.

(Transport must be provided for occasions such as these.)

Coach outings to the sea or favourite beauty spots.

Invitations (for the mobile) to school open days and fêtes.

Instrumental groups to play in the Old People's Homes. Residents who have in the past played an instrument may be invited to join the group.

Organised visits to the theatre or pantomime.

4. *Service*

A wide range of activities can be covered:

Shopping for those who are shut in, or for those who, though able to get out, are unable to carry a heavy basket.

Some forms of outdoor work: sweeping up leaves; shovelling away snow; mowing the lawn; putting out dustbins for the refuse collection; chopping wood.

(Pupils should guard against doing heavy manual work as a *regular* thing. There may be the occasional need to do some strenuous digging or weeding.)

Minor repairs around the house.

Major repairs and decorating may become an organised project for a group during the holidays (e.g. Groups of girls have sometimes helped decorate parts of the Peckham Union of Girls' Schools' Settlement during their holidays).

Exchanging library books for the shut-ins.

Keeping a circulation of novels, magazines, *Reader's Digest* going amongst the old folk.

Pushing those in wheel-chairs around parks, etc., on summer days immediately after school.

Darning and mending for those whose sight is failing.

CHILDREN

1. *Regular visits*

Visiting children in a children's home (e.g. under the local authority). Again, it should be stressed that the visits must be regular. If they are not, they only add to the child's insecurity.

2. *Parties*

One school gave a Christmas party for the children from two local homes, and organised it as a Red Indian party. All the hostesses were dressed as squaws. The hall was decorated with wigwams, imitation camp fires, totem-poles, etc., and the children were divided into tribes for the various games. Before the children left, each home was presented with a large, gay wigwam to be shared by all the children.

3. *Picnics and Outings*
It is advisable to arrange that for every child there is one pupil personally responsible for his care throughout the day once they have left the coach. Where expenses are likely to be incurred, e.g. for ice creams at the seaside, or rides on miniature trains, etc., it is best to provide each pupil with some money in advance, and stress that they must not spend wildly beyond that sum and expect remuneration. On one occasion the girls in a school made individual purses for each of the children from the homes invited on an outing, and embroidered the name of each child on his/her purse. Then 25p was put into each purse so that the children could buy without having to ask their hostesses for money. It was touching to note that some of them spent part of their money on presents for those who were looking after them.

4. *Gifts*
Christmas presents. Easter eggs. Birthday presents and cards. (Stress that if this is done for one it must be done for every child.)

5. *Letters*
When contact has been established, through an outing or a party, it is a good idea to continue this with occasional but regular letters, since children in homes receive very few letters. A suitable birthday present might include writing paper, envelopes and a book of stamps, so that they are free to reply if they wish.

6. *Projects*
If the homes are near by, it may be possible for groups of pupils to make regular visits and work on a particular project with the children, either following a hobby or a topic of interest, or producing a play or pantomime. Again, the important thing is the continuity.

7. *Play*
Where there are hospitals for disabled or subnormal children who are permanent or semi-permanent patients, pupils from local

schools are sometimes encouraged to attach themselves to a particular ward and provide a rota of visitors to play with the children each day after school. It is essential to prepare pupils adequately before sending them to work amongst such children so that, in the initial visits, they are not unduly shocked or distressed by the experience. Most of the secondary schools in the Sutton Local Education Authority, for example, participate in such a scheme and visit the wards of Queen Mary's Hospital for Children at Carshalton. Besides daily visits they also take an active part in the annual fête and contribute financial help in other ways. With a special liaison officer to co-ordinate the work of volunteers from the schools, it has been possible to arrange for fifth form pupils to work on the wards full time during the weeks following their O level examinations before starting the sixth form courses.

HANDICAPPED CHILDREN

Where there are schools or homes for physically and mentally handicapped children, many of the above ideas may be applied. Friendship and practical help in letter-writing, wheeling chairs, assisting in swimming lessons, outings, etc., are greatly appreciated.

The organisation

The responsibilities of the R.E. teacher range over such a wide area (the teaching itself, social service activities, the arranging of assemblies, fostering the work of the Christian Society in the school) that sometimes one feels more like a juggler trying to keep all the balls in the air than a teacher. If the social service activities are to fulfil their proper function, it is essential to have a good and efficient committee that can help organise the different aspects of the work, and keep in constant touch with what is going on. It is impossible for one or even two members of staff to keep a check on all the visitors to ensure that they are going regularly to their old people or children. All needy cases requiring follow-up should be reported to the staff members, but occasional routine checks should be carried out by the pupil committee members themselves.

Trustworthy sixth formers are capable of counting money as it comes in from collections and fêtes, though the staff member must be responsible for the final check and banking of it.

A highly efficient filing system is necessary so that useful names and addresses are readily available: old people in the area; children's homes; remand homes; orphanages with which the school is in contact; all the national organisations and charities supported by the school; the local welfare and children's officers; local priests and ministers; organisers of such services as W.V.S. and Meals on Wheels, etc. Records should also be kept of all pupils participating in any social service activity. Amounts of money sent to various good causes will, of course, appear in the accounts, but details of how the money was raised and by whom should also be kept. There should also be full details of any special fund-raising project with comments as to its success or failure and an evaluation of it as a method.

Fund-raising efforts will vary enormously from school to school. Spot collections are popular for emergency appeals, e.g. for earthquake or flood victims. Bob-a-job efforts may continue throughout the school year with car-cleaning, book-binding, cupboard tidying, etc. Cake and sweet stalls, white elephant stalls and jumble sales never fail to raise satisfactory sums of money. Charity football or basketball matches are also very popular.

Not all schools, however, will be able to organise fund-raising activities, but pupils can still be encouraged to make practical contributions, e.g.a blanket knitting competition to see which forms can produce the most blankets out of knitted squares within a given time. These blankets are very acceptable to some old people and needy families. Geriatric wards are also very grateful for them. Similar competitions can be arranged for the making of soft toys, small knitted garments, crocheted ponchos, etc., for distribution to local families (on the advice of the local welfare officer) or for organisations such as Save the Children Fund, Christian Aid, TEAR Fund, and Oxfam, and for boys it may be possible to make and sell small household objects out of odd scraps of wood or metal. With one bag of cement, an old dustbin lid as a mould and some wire meshing it is possible to make a very attractive pedestal bird-bath that would sell at between two and three pounds.

One of the most important supervisory duties of the R.E. teacher is to see that no pupil takes on more than he can reasonably tackle without homework or health suffering. If staff as a whole complain that there has been a serious decline in a pupil's work, then it is advisable to check up on the amount of time being spent in social service. There may be no relation between the two, but sometimes pupils are not able to apportion their energies wisely. In girls' schools, in particular, there is a need for liaison with the parents so that they know what their daughters are doing and when they are likely to be home later than usual.

It is important to spread the load of social service work throughout the whole of the secondary school. Sometimes the activities beyond the school in the local community are thought suitable only for senior pupils, but often first- and second-year pupils make very good visitors. They may even be slightly less inhibited than older pupils. Provided they go in pairs and are given encouragement and proper supervision they can take a full share in the school's care for the old folk. The programmes for work amongst children are probably better carried out by more senior pupils, especially in the case of the sub-normal or handicapped.

In many areas there are joint schools' committees to co-ordinate the social service activities and avoid overlapping. The R.E. teacher or a senior member of the school social service committee should keep in touch and work in close co-operation with the co-ordinating body as also with organisations such as Task Force and the Community Service Volunteers. It is a good way of sharing ideas and useful information, and a further way of forging links with neighbouring schools.

Links between practical and classroom work

With fifth and sixth form groups it may be possible to link the following kind of teaching material with the interest in practical work. Many of these suggestions appear in one section or another of the various R.E. syllabuses.

PROBLEMS

1. *Hunger*

Food production and distribution, the causes and cures of world hunger, the consequences of malnutrition, the need for generosity and 'being given to hospitality' in the widest sense, the teaching of Jesus on sharing.

2. *Poverty*

The nature of poverty and what it does to the dignity of man, and the dignity of family life: the moral, social and health problems resulting from overcrowding and inadequate housing; the concern of Jesus for the poor (e.g. the story of the rich young ruler who was instructed to give to the poor) and his own involvement in poverty ('Foxes have holes and birds of the air have their nests, but the Son of Man hath not where to lay his head'); the instructions of Jesus to his disciples to 'travel light' with one coat, one pair of sandals, etc., and not to become too attached to material things (and the Franciscan continuation of this).

Illustrate the concern of the early Christians for their poorer brethren: the famine relief fund from Antioch to Jerusalem; early practice of Christian 'communism'; the sharing of food at the agape feast and Paul's rebuke at the display of greed by some; the 'collection' taken up by the churches in Greece and Macedonia for the Jerusalem church.

3. *Loneliness*

The problems of loneliness amongst: old people; young people; drop-outs and misfits of society; outcasts from society by virtue of their past reputation, nationality, some abnormality or perversion, unmarried status, e.g. the lonely bachelor, middle-aged spinster, unmarried mother, widow or widower, etc.

Study the work of the Samaritans, Darby and Joan Clubs, Youth Clubs, Lonely Hearts Clubs, and examine the ways in which the Church is meeting (or not meeting) the needs of many lonely people. How may we recognise loneliness?

4. *Dependence on drugs, alcohol, meths., smoking, gambling, witchcraft*

Discuss the possible reasons behind the dependence. Does it indicate that a search is going on? If so, for what or for whom? What is our responsibility? Discuss the work of: Sally Trench, *Bury me in my Boots*; David Wilkerson, *The Cross and the Switchblade*; Alcoholics Anonymous; Gamblers Anonymous.

Talk about the care of alcoholics and drug addicts at Spelthorne St. Mary near Egham, Surrey (run by the Sisters of the Community of St. Mary the Virgin) and the group therapy work of St. Bernard's Hospital, Southall, Middlesex (there may be other treatment centres nearer to the school that could be cited as examples of care); the efforts of such organisations as the Church of England Moral Welfare Society; the rescue work and rehabilitation work of the Salvation Army.

5. *Suffering*

historical survey showing the ways in which Christian thinking prompted social reform through:

Charles Dickens;	Robert Raikes;
William Wilberforce;	John Pounds;

Lord Shaftesbury;	F. D. Maurice and Charles Kingsley;
Dr. Barnardo;	William Booth.
Elizabeth Fry;	

Make a study of the work being done by both Christian and secular bodies to alleviate suffering, e.g.:

Imperial Cancer Research	Christian Aid;
Muscular Dystrophy Society;	Pestalozzi Villages;
Shelter;	Ockenden Venture;
Refuge;	Save the Children Fund;
Oxfam;	TEAR Fund.

7

BEYOND THE CLASSROOM

A book with the title *Approaches to Religious Education* has necessarily dealt mainly with ideas for the classroom and their implementation, and throughout it has been heavily biased towards the teaching of R.E. in secondary schools, though I hope some of the material and ideas will prove useful to primary school teachers too. This final chapter is, however, quite specifically for those R.E. specialists in secondary education who see their role in much wider terms than simply as teacher of a subject which is begun, continued and ended in the classroom. In actual fact there would be very few conscientious teachers of any subject who would think in that way, for the pupil/teacher relationship is fostered and nurtured in numerous small ways beyond the actual lessons. For the R.E. specialist, however, there are particularly important opportunities and pastoral responsibilities.

Counselling and pastoral work

There is an increasing awareness in schools today of the need for those able and skilled in counselling. With the great emphasis on the totality of education to be offered, it is clear that the deepest needs of children are not met by simply feeding the mind and catering for physical development. There are emotional and spiritual needs which in adolescence often loom larger than intellectual needs. With a decline in church-going there is a greater need than ever for pastoral help to be available at school. At one time, young people might have turned to a youth leader, Sunday School teacher, Guide captain, priest or minister. When a very large group of fourteen-year-old girls was asked to list in order of priority the people they would turn to in real trouble, clergy and ministers did not feature very high up, if at all, on their lists. In a large number of cases parents also came fairly low down. Surprisingly a fair percentage said that they would confide in a teacher. I say surprisingly because it is a mark of the extent to which the staff/student relationships have lost some of their rigidity and stiff formality.

Recognising the need for specialist training and qualifications in counselling, there are a number of universities which offer one- or two-year courses of training, or courses may be followed at the Tavistock Institute. If teachers do not feel able to take a year's leave of absence, they may perhaps consider following a course in Clinical Theology* in their evenings. It is a helpful training in the art of listening and recognising the symptomatic behaviour of certain personality patterns as well as leading to greater self-knowledge, which, painful as it may be, is a most salutary part of one's training as a counsellor.

A number of schools now offer posts for counsellors as full-time jobs. Others ask that counselling should be combined with a little teaching. The system of full-time counsellors has both its advantages and disadvantages. In spite of his specialised training, as well as the fair overall information he may have on every pupil by reference to academic and medical reports, personal dossiers, and preferences in choice of careers, the counsellor still may not have enough personal contact with pupils. Often his work involves advising in matters of careers, applications to university and colleges of education (together with filling in UCCA forms), liaison with the welfare officer, school doctor and sundry other ancillary helpers. He may also be involved in home visits and parent/teacher relationships. All of this is vastly important, and might well lighten the load of the hard-pressed house master or mistress in the comprehensive school, or form teacher in the secondary school (though they would probably not wish to be relieved of all their pastoral duties), but it may not leave a great deal of time for the interviews with individual pupils. Naturally,

* Clinical Theology Association, 'Lingdale', Weston Avenue, Mount Hooton Road, Nottingham.

the job is what the counsellor makes it, and if availability to deal with personal problems ranks as the priority, then his accessibility will come first and his function in the school will be enormously valuable.

Many schools do not have counsellors as such, but every form teacher has the opportunity to fill some of the counsellor's role. It is his duty to keep a watchful eye on all pupils in his class and to be aware of physical and emotional stresses which might affect the child's work. Sometimes the Head or parent entrust the form teacher with very personal knowledge of family disruptions and upheavals, financial crises and other problems, if it is felt essential to share such knowledge with one so closely concerned with the pupil's welfare. The necessary personal attention relating to subject choices (when selection has to be made), curriculum arrangements and practical difficulties in coping with homework, travelling, financial pressures, etc., are usually the concern of the form teacher, who normally has at least one opportunity during the year for a lengthy discussion with the parents of each pupil. This is good and indicates the growing ease in relationship between the parents, teachers and pupils. But there is still a very particular function for the R.E. teacher.

Even with all the official provision of counselling help, it may not meet the whole need. It is not always possible to share personal matters with someone because he happens to be officially appointed to deal with them. The factor of personality enters into it, and we find it easier to share with some people than others, though it may have nothing to do with trust or worthiness.

Sometimes it is very difficult to open up on personal problems in 'cold blood' as it were, in isolation from the lesson or discussion in which the problems surfaced. Often questions come as a natural follow-on from a lesson and are addressed to the particular subject teacher involved. If he has secured the trust of his pupils, he will quite readily become their pastoral dustbin. For example, Biology teachers are often entrusted with confidences of teenagers and asked for advice (by girls particularly) about the disturbing emotional and physical signs of puberty. Nowadays they may also, regrettably, want to know in confidence how to get on to the pill or off a drug.

R.E. lessons are, by their very nature, likely to bring into focus questions of personal relationships, the future of our world, life after death, faith and unbelief. Sometimes the questions of pupils follow directly on a lesson, but more often than not they come later. The questioner may be searching for ultimate truths, wanting to probe deeper than the lesson allowed, either because of the time limit or because of the inhibiting presence of other members of the class. The subject matter of a particular lesson may have touched upon a very tender area and triggered off a host of reactions, or even broken open an old wound. Occasionally one has evidences of just how penetrating the Bible can be when one is seeking to help those who have been bowled over by a particular lesson. How easy it is to launch into a study of Hosea without first checking if there are any in that form whose home life has been shattered by unfaithfulness and desertion. I shall never forget the ghastly occasion when a girl rushed from my sixth form class shaking with convulsive sobs. I had taken a series of four lessons on the problem of suffering, using Job as background material. This was the third lesson and no one had told me that the girl's father was in the last stages of cancer. I had not thought to consult with the form teacher before tackling the whole problem of suffering, and it made me realise afresh how vulnerable pupils can be in some lessons. It is a great help if the Head alerts the R.E. teacher of known cases where divorce, separation or death are imminent, so that he can tread very tenderly and sensitively in those areas that are likely to be painful, and steer discussion away from subjects that would twist the knife in an open wound. It is impossible always to avoid subjects which may be painful to certain pupils, but a real knowledge of them and their backgrounds, a deep insight and constant awareness that it is possible to blunder very clumsily into private grief will guard a teacher from making the sort of mistake I made. Conversely it helps to discuss problems which are particular to some pupils in a general and objective way, but the golden rule is to know one's class individually.

Besides questions relating to boy friends, and rows with parents (which may be dealt with by any sympathetic member of staff), pupils often seek the advice of the R.E. specialist over amateur dabblings in spiritualism, table tappings and levitation. The ouija board may have had scary things to say, and they desperately want assurance that 'there's nothing in it really'. They normally come to the R.E. specialist because they expect him to have an opinion, and let us hope it is always given in no uncertain terms! It is a good thing, therefore, for the R.E. teacher to take a turn round the school buildings occasionally during a lunch hour just to be obviously and easily accessible. A pupil who finds it difficult to initiate conversation with a teacher can do so more easily by catching him informally in the corridor, rather than having to make a special appointment. It is important to realise that the opening remark or question may not be the real question at all; it is often just a way of capturing attention and beginning some sort of conversation. We all employ this ruse, so we should be able to recognise it in others. There is a great need for selflessness over the lunch hour. One is tempted to guard it jealously as precious 'time off' for relaxation (and so it often should be), but when pupils come from far afield and have to rush off after school to catch buses and trains, it is frequently the only time when they are able to chat informally to staff. Sometimes one can arrange to meet a pupil at the end of the afternoon, or possibly even get away from school premises altogether, though *To Sir, with Love* should be a reminder to exercise utmost discretion here.

Experienced teachers will be aware of the following points, but for newcomers it may be helpful to mention some of the difficulties.

Often in already overcrowded school buildings there is no room where a member of staff can meet a pupil to talk privately, and yet often one does need privacy and a guarantee that one will not be disturbed. Odd corners along corridors, balconies in the assembly hall, prep rooms, cupboards, all manner of strange places have to serve this purpose. In the summer it is possible to get outside, perhaps, but to be seen in deep conversation with a pupil arouses the curiosity not only of the other pupils but of the staff too. Not meaning to strain confidence colleagues sometimes enquire, 'You were having a long heart to heart with so-and-so; what on earth was it all about?' And one has to be politely evasive.

Which brings us to the next point: the need for a guarded tongue and in some cases sealed lips. Often when pupils come to talk, what they have to say is in the nature of a confession, and whilst the unloading may be done in an informal way, it *must* have upon it the absolute seal of the confessional. This occasionally leads to a conflict of loyalties for the teacher, when something which has been disclosed concerns school administration or some crisis in staff/student relationship. Loyalty to one's Head makes one long to shed the load, but the only course possible is to persuade the pupil as strongly as wisdom permits to take the matter to the Head himself. Never must confidence be destroyed. One or two specific examples may serve to show the kind of problems that may be revealed to a teacher, and the dilemma in which a counselling situation may place him. A pupil may admit to being on drugs, or knowing that others are on drugs. If this information is shared in confidence, what should the teacher do? His responsibility is divided between the pupil, the Head and the parents. It is not simply doctors who are faced with the ethical problem as to whether or not they should disclose certain facts to parents, for example, that their son is taking drugs or their daughter is on the pill. A teacher (especially a very young and inexperienced one) may wonder how far he is right to shoulder the full burden of this knowledge.

A parent may in confidence inform a teacher of homosexual or black magic activities taking place in a school. Is the parent, in fact, hoping that without his identity being revealed and his child being questioned the matter will be taken to the Head, or does he hope that the teacher will, on his own initiative, take the necessary steps to check the activities?

If a child has confessed to a teacher that he has been engaging in petty thefts, and the Head has been aware not only of the problem but has carried out various searches and has had his suspicions about a pupil who is not in fact the offender, what should the teacher do? Obviously he should try and persuade the culprit to own up to the Head, but what if he refuses? Must the teacher remain dumb?

There are no easy answers to these questions. There are no right and wrong solutions, for every such problem must be settled in the light of the variables in the situation in the relationship between staff and Headmaster, pupils and Headmaster, whether or not the pupil came to unburden once only, or in the hope that the teacher would pave the way for his fuller admission to the Head.

The teacher needs to be discerning enough to distinguish between genuine truth, exaggerations or distortions of the truth and downright lies. He needs to judge whether the pupil has come running to spill over in a moment of panic, or if this is a problem that has been troubling him deeply for some time and which at last he has brought himself to share.

Whichever way the teacher decides to act he will probably suffer agonies of indecision but it is an inescapable tension. Often, however, there are unexpected and touching compensations in the ways in which pupils show their sincere gratitude.

To become the confidante of a pupil (at least, in a girls' school) can have somewhat trying consequences. A girl with a strongly hysteric type of personality may become too dependent, lean so heavily upon the teacher, and demand so much attention, that she becomes an embarrassment and at times a little bit of a nuisance. The teacher may really desire to show all the loving care so greatly needed, but, apart from being unable to give a disproportionate amount of time to one of many pupils, does not feel able to put up with the constant tappings on the staff-room door with the plea to talk to Miss . . . It not only becomes a talking point in the staff-room (and a most unwelcome interruption at times) but also tends to make the girl very suspect among her classmates. Again, great caution and wisdom is needed in counselling such pupils, and very particularly in mixed schools, but firmness with kindness usually keeps the thing in a right perspective. It is advisable to keep a slightly detached air at first, and to restrain oneself from showing sympathy through physical contact, e.g. putting arms around shoulders of sobbing girls etc., to avoid embarrassment on either side later (though there is always a peculiar bond after shared confidences). It must also be recognised that if a girl is always seeking the attention of a member of staff, however odd it may seem, it is a cry for help, and every effort should be made to sift out the underlying problem.

There are times when pupils come to unburden themselves and

then, having done so, do not come again. This usually means that they have found the necessary relief and perhaps the advice given was right and the problem has been resolved. It is a good thing, however, to stop and chat to such pupils on casual meetings, not *necessarily* about the former occasion but just to reassure them that you have not forgotten them or their problems, even if they no longer need or ask for help. Sometimes there is a real follow-up work to be done in counselling and if the teacher has volunteered to look into some matter, then, at all costs, it must be done. Failure to do so would again reduce or even destroy confidence.

Counselling is an exacting part of the work of an R.E. teacher, but a vital one. Many and varied are the problems which are shared, so that perhaps if one was allowed to choose which gift of the Holy Spirit one would covet most, it would be the gift of wisdom.

One last word of warning. Success in the realm of counselling and R.E. in general will inevitably mean misunderstanding, perhaps ill feeling and even rank opposition from some quarters. It happens, as Jesus warned us quite unequivocally that it would, though that does not always take the sting out of it when it does. However, much can be done to keep harmonious relationships in the staff room if the R.E. teacher shows every possible consideration to colleagues and a prodigality of generosity in the give and take of school life. Never to forget to consult those who should be consulted, or even those who would be hurt not to be consulted; always to prepare gently before launching bombshells; to make extra efforts to talk to and communicate with one's critics, can temper the steel in the heart. It will never be entirely smooth, however, for it is not really the R.E. teacher who is under attack but the Gospel he represents.

The Student Christian Group

It is a matter of real importance that the R.E. teacher should take a sympathetic interest in the activities of the Christian Union or C.E.M. group. Often groups (even if affiliated to the larger national organisations of C.E.M. or I.S.C.F.) have non-sectarian names such as The Christian Fellowship, Agape, Forum, etc., and this is usually a diplomatic move, but even if the school group is run on lines or affiliated to an organisation that would not have been the teacher's own choice, this should not excuse an R.E. teacher from offering every encouragement and support within his power. It would be tragic if a school countenanced two rival groups, but if such an unfortunate state of affairs existed, then the R.E. teacher should try and support both.

Although the leadership of these groups should be, and usually is, in the hands of the senior pupils, there is a quite definite need for staff support in the background, and the advice and wisdom that can be offered from experience. One of the reasons why Christian groups are sometimes unpopular and often suspect in a school is that there has been little guidance and direction from staff members, and the group, though deeply zealous, has been unwise in some of its extremist approaches. In their enthusiasm and youthful fervour, student committees sometimes regard staff advice as far too moderate and cautious, but they do not always see how needful it is to be 'as wise as serpents and harmless as doves'.

It may seem very elementary, but committees often need considerable help in simple practical matters of running a society. They certainly need the stimulus of ideas to provide an attractive and balanced programme, and they look to staff members of the committee (if they are on the committee) to suggest speakers. There is sometimes a need for a certain amount of training in writing letters of invitation to prospective speakers. Often a newly appointed secretary will write a very bald letter, simply giving the date, time and subject of the meeting and ask if the person concerned is free to come. It helps if the R.E. teacher can 'check' the letters at first (without it seeming to take the responsibility out of student hands) to ensure that more information is given, such as average attendance at the group meeting, the age-range, whether or not the majority are committed Christians with a church background, or whether it is a group which draws a number of those with no Christian connections. It is helpful to the speaker, too, to know if there is to be time for questions, and whether or not the meetings open and/or close with a devotional act. In my experience pupils often spring it upon a speaker that they will 'now close with prayer', and they should be made fully aware that this is neither right nor fair. Chairing a meeting is never easy at first, and the art of doing it graciously and giving just the appropriate amount of information about a speaker when introducing him, and a sincere but adequate word of thanks at the end, is something which needs a lot of practice. There are not all that many occasions in school life when pupils receive such training. Furthermore, it is regrettable that speakers are not always met and welcomed as they should be. It can be very confusing to find one's way into and around a large school building, and it is always most reassuring for a visiting speaker to find a reception committee of perhaps two pupils, waiting to meet and greet him, show him to the cloakroom (often a forgotten factor), introduce him to the Head (if this is the normal practice in the school) and fill in any gaps of knowledge that the letters of invitation have not covered for the ease and smooth running of the meeting.

Most Christian groups do not have very much money in their funds, but if they are expecting speakers to travel some distance to address them, then they ought to offer to pay expenses. Many people would decline such help, but as part of their training the committee, and especially the treasurer, should not only be reminded that this should be done on every occasion, but given some advice as to how to approach a rather delicate subject tactfully.

Then there are the 'thank-you' letters afterwards. These little courtesies of receiving and welcoming speakers, thanking them adequately on the spot, offering them their expenses, and then following up the visit with a thank-you letter are not only important as part of the training of the pupils but they are also much appreciated by the speakers, who have given generously of their time. I knew one minister who had spoken at many C.U. meetings in schools and colleges and finally refused to accept any more invitations on the grounds that students were often *so* casual about the organisation of the meetings (on one occasion no room had been arranged) and everything was taken for granted, including his petrol. Sometimes he had travelled quite long distances to speak at lunch-time university meetings but there had never been any question as to whether or not he had had, or would be able to get some lunch himself. Unfortunately this is not an isolated case. In groups that are specifically labelled 'Christian' there should never be any presuming upon the charity of those who often have to budget very carefully in both time and money.

Staff help is most especially appreciated in programme planning. Even if a committee is able to produce a fund of good ideas, it is not always confident that it can see them through unaided.

It is important first that the aims of the group are clear. Does it exist simply to provide fellowship and nourishment for the committed Christians? If so, then the programme is pretty straightforward. One would hope, however, that its raison d'être would not be only to offer a cosy little Bible study for the faithful but to provide a public platform where topical and controversial issues could be given an airing, and Christian attitudes and ethics seen as relevant to these situations providing answers that will satisfy at many different levels. The R.E. teacher can help the committee to see that the programme is varied and balanced and does not duplicate or supplement the R.E. syllabus, otherwise it becomes simply another lesson. There are many important issues and questions that young people raise, which often through lack of time are not necessarily covered by the R.E. syllabus, e.g. questions of medical ethics, and differing reactions to genetical research and modern surgery; issues being raised in the Commons dealing with such problems as race relations and immigration; the imprisonment of Church leaders for their active engagement in politics in South Africa and behind the Iron Curtain; pollution; population explosion; the 'Brave New World'; and Christian commitment and discipleship.

Thus the programme should have a wide appeal to any in the school who think seriously about human problems and issues, and who are trying to formulate responsible attitudes towards them. This is not to say that the programme should have such a popular appeal that it is simply a form of lunch-time entertainment which has nothing positive to say, neither stirring people deeply nor challenging them to consider the Christian claims and viewpoints.

Sometimes it is a good thing to invite local clergy and ministers as speakers, since it is of mutual help that they should have the chance of meeting young people in but not of their parishes, and also that pupils should be able to see for themselves that, behind the dog-collars, clergy are very human, and not quite the blundering if lovable idiots of *All Gas and Gaiters*. Bringing clergy into the school also helps to reinforce the fact of the Church's concern with young people, social problems and political issues, and the practical steps that Christian groups are taking to help and serve in the community.

Senior pupils love a Brains Trust type of programme in which various members of the staff are invited to take part. They enjoy listening to members of staff putting forward opposing viewpoints and sometimes engaging in heated discussion. With older pupils it is a healthy thing for them to see a confrontation between, for example, a Christian and a Humanist, provided both stand firmly by their convictions, and don't bend over backwards to try and give the impression that 'we're saying the same things really only we just use a different terminology!' Discussions of this nature need ruthless honesty, and are not to be feared, but great care is needed in the choice of speakers. It is essential that both sides in any debate should be presented fairly and well, since at that age, pupils might not be able to distinguish between a weakly presented case and a weak cause.

It is never pleasant to harry pupils, but it pays dividends to do this over the question of publicity. If notices are well designed, bold and attractive *and* displayed well in advance of the meeting, it makes a most favourable impression of both enthusiasm and efficiency. If the publicity officer is dilatory it can reduce the attendance at meetings alarmingly. Sincere Christian pupils are often greatly concerned about their witness in a school. Let them know that possibly the most effective witness is that of zeal coupled with a business-like approach.

The other function of the staff adviser to the Christian group is that of liaison between the Head, the rest of the staff and the group. Invitations to take part in meetings should be made by a direct approach of the committee to the staff concerned, but sometimes when there are complaints or misunderstandings the staff adviser can act as mediator or buffer.

It is often necessary to check the contacts made and invitations which go out to groups in other schools. An unsuspecting committee can land itself into very bad odour by not observing the correct etiquette. It needs also to be reminded constantly that the caretaker must be notified of all meetings and activities. Often where there has been a lapse, the staff member has to pacify a very irate caretaker whose cleaners have been halted in their work.

Arranging joint conferences with the schools in the area needs considerable help from staff to check that *all* necessary arrangements have been made, permissions granted and suitable invitations issued.

These are just simple practical details, but so easily forgotten, even by staff, and yet it is most important that a Christian group should be business-like, efficient and considerate to all likely to be affected by their activities.

Above all, the R.E. teacher should help to keep the members of the group alive to opportunities of service within the school, befriending the lonely, encouraging the down-hearted, entering bravely into discussion with those who despise and oppose what they do not understand. In every community there are the outcasts and the unwanted, the bullies and the cheats, those of twisted minds and perverted humour, together with the sensitive, emotionally maimed, innocent, generous and heroic characters (and most of us have some of all these ingredients in us). If the Christian group can be thoroughly outgoing to all in selfless love and giving, then it will be doing far more to the glory of God than all the attractive programmes and superb publicity would ever achieve.

Quiet days and retreats

One of the most encouraging features in the field of religious education is the growing demand for quiet days and retreats amongst senior pupils. It is not all that new a venture for public schools, schools of Anglican or Roman Catholic foundations or those run by religious communities, but, if one scans the list of retreat bookings in *Vision*,* it is interesting to see what a variety of school and college groups are represented. Some of them are pre-confirmation retreats booked by the chaplains of public schools, some are quiet days for C.U. or C.E.M. groups, a number of G.P.D.S.T. schools arrange annual retreats for their senior girls, but there are also bookings from grammar schools, secondary modern schools and comprehensive schools of local education authorities, as well as some retreats primarily reserved for teachers.

This increase in demand for retreats is significant. It is not that they are being imposed by fanatical teachers of the Catholic wing of the Church, though even if this were the case, it would not diminish their value! It is simply that the need for periods of silence and rest is increasingly being felt by people of all brands of churchmanship and even no churchmanship at all. The Maharishi Mahesh Yogi has popularised the value of meditation for inner composure, and more and more people (including young people) are recognising the need to balance our strenuous activism with periods of contemplation. The kind of retreats run by religious communities and retreat houses of the A.P.R.† are, of course, spiritual retreats which provide the necessary silence and devotional leadership to get centred on God. The buildings are often designed or even purpose built to make the keeping of silence easy and natural. In the case of school retreats rules are often adapted so that there are some short periods of talking each day (perhaps at meals). It may seem an alarming prospect to arrange a quiet day or retreat, yet it need hold no terrors! One's own fears must never stand in the way of the needs of one's pupils.

Most people feel very nervous before their first retreat, and wonder if they will forget and burst into conversation, or find it all too much and be reduced to helpless giggles. Such fears are usually totally unfounded. The houses so lend themselves to silence, and

* *Vision*, the official half-yearly journal of the Assocation for Promoting Retreats.

† The Association for Promoting Retreats, Church House, Newton Road, London W2 5LS.

the atmosphere is such that there is no urge to chatter, and often one's thinking reaches a level where one would greatly regret any disturbance. However, it is often a good thing to train oneself to go into silence by degrees, starting with a day of quiet, and then progressing later to a weekend retreat or even longer.

For a school group it is relatively easy to arrange a quiet day using the premises of a local church. When we tried this, in one school in which I was teaching, we found that at least two of the local churches (one an Anglican and the other a Baptist) were delighted to give us the free run of their buildings. In fact, one church arranged for some of their lady members to cater for us, and they served a superb lunch and tea at an extraordinarily low price. Small rooms were available for those who chose to sit around in easy chairs to read or meditate, but most preferred to spend the time in the church itself. Throughout the day, the minister's vestry was available for interviews and counselling by the conductor, and this is a very important point to remember in arranging such days. When one enters into a period of silence with God, he is likely to have some disturbing things to say, things that have been consistently repressed in the business of normal living. So it is essential to have help available if needed.

We were very fortunate in that, although we were fully prepared to meet the expenses for the hire of the rooms and church, the clergy concerned refused to accept any payment saying, 'This is what we exist for'. It made it considerably easier to encourage girls to come, of course, because besides giving up a day of their half-term holiday, there were travelling expenses and their meals to cover. In the half-term experiment (we had previously held two quiet days during term time on Saturdays and had used the school premises) twenty-four girls came and their ages ranged from fourteen to eighteen. The programme which we followed was a very simple one, not leaving too long a stretch of silence at any one time, since we did not want to overtax or deter the younger pupils. The older pupils could have done with more silence, but at least it gave them a taste for a longer retreat.

The following outline will give some idea of the breakdown of the day:

10.00–10.15	Coffee and exploration of the building to discover the 'geography' of the place. All rooms clearly labelled.
10.15–10.30	Introductory talk and devotions.
10.30–11.15	First talk: followed by any immediate questions for elucidation.
11.15–12.30	Silence.
12.30– 1.30	Lunch and free time for brief walk, etc.
1.30– 2.15	Second talk: followed by necessary questions for elucidation.
2.15– 3.30	Silence.
3.30– 3.45	Tea.
3.45– 4.30	A session of sharing thoughts, insights, etc., and any further questions arising from the day's thinking.
4.30– 5.00	Closing act of devotion.

In preparing the group for the day, and in the introductory talk, the following points were made so that the pupils would get the maximum benefit and enjoyment from it.

Do not strain after great mystical experiences, or worry if you do not feel particularly holy nor have any uplifting thoughts. Simply try and relax completely. You are just offering this day as a gift to God and putting yourself utterly at his disposal. If he has things to say, then he will have a chance to say them to you, for you are going to try and give him your undivided attention. Sometimes in silence he says rather disturbing things to us, and you may feel the need to talk and ask advice. The conductor will be in the vestry and will be willing to talk to you if you need to share your concern. Do not spend too long looking at yourself. You may need to do this for a while, and then having made confession, turn your eyes and spend the rest of the time looking at God. Whatever he has to give you, be assured he will give it; he can pour in as much of his grace as you need, despite the shortness of time.

Think of it as a day spent with a friend; you are hoping just to enjoy the company of that friend without interruption of routine daily duties and other friends. It may turn out to be just a very nice day in which you enjoy each other's company enormously. On the other hand, it may be a very important day in which you take great strides forward in your relationship. Whatever happens, just accept it and be thankful for what God is giving you. Do not strain for what you think you *should* have; God in his wisdom knows just what we need. If the silence becomes too oppressive for you, then go and talk to one of the staff members or give a friend the *suivez-moi* look, and get out for a short walk and chat. You are meant to enjoy the silence and feel it wrapping you round like a soft and comforting blanket. It should not turn into a kind of endurance test!

Take a notebook and pencil, for as you think, read or meditate, there may be thoughts and questions which you would like to ponder and pursue further at another time, and have by you a helpful devotional book to which you can turn if you feel you are 'drying up'.

Do not feel guilty if, at first, you sit and do nothing, neither reading, praying, meditating nor even consciously thinking. The 'nothingness' is a necessary part of the letting go and entering into the inner stillness. You certainly do not need to fill up the day with non-stop chatter to God.

In the quiet days which we held amongst these girls, there was no apparent strain. None seemed particularly threatened by the silence, and obviously it was enjoyed so much by some that they wish to continue having regular retreats.

Besides the above points it is as well in arranging a quiet day to have a collection of devotional books, biographies of saints, etc., on loan in an accessible place (Retreat Houses have their own libraries) and ensure a wide enough range of material to cater for the different age-groups. There are a number of useful booklets on how to enjoy retreats published by the A.P.R. Some small notebooks and pencils should also be on sale for those who need them.

One idea, borrowed from the Darmstadt Sisters, is to have a tray with a selection of cards (be sure of one for each) on which is written a special text or exhortation. These are placed face downwards and each retreatant takes one card from the tray at the beginning of the quiet day and takes this as God's special word to him or her. He need not share it with anyone else.

Sometimes it is possible to join an already arranged open or parish retreat; there are usually some vacancies for extra retreatants. This is perhaps not such a good idea if, for most of the pupils, it is the first experience of a retreat. It might help them to be more relaxed if the retreat centre were booked for the school group only. There would then be no fear of intruding upon others or disturbing the more experienced retreatants.

The value of these quiet days and retreats is inestimable. To have helped educate young people into a love of silence is a far more worthwhile lesson to take into adult life than many of the lessons of the classroom. '. . . the realisation of the value of silence is a moment of true spiritual discovery in their lives. It is the awakening of a thirst that will never leave them, the thirst for silence—"la fontaine qui coule où personne ne passe; mais Dieu y vient boire".*'† The pace of life often bewilders young people and is partly responsible for the drop-outs. Can one wonder that sometimes they want to cry out 'Stop the world, I want to get off!'? In the midst of so much speed and competition, the spirit has no time to be still and know God, the ground and centre of our beings. It used to be said that the Sahara had a vast ocean beneath it which was impossible to tap. Life is sometimes like a dreary and dusty desert. The oceans of God's living water are there, but we can't get through. The silence of a retreat enables the surface of our lives to get in touch with the depths underneath and to find springs of water welling up.

It is important, too, in days when young people are so anxious to express their concern for the needy in community service, to impress upon them that the offering to God of time in silence is as acceptable and as important as the offerings of money and activity. The reforms of the great prophetic movements of history have all begun with contemplation and the hearing of the 'still, small voice'. A wave must always retreat before it can advance!

The value of such retreats in terms of group relationships and staff/student relationships is incalculable. Silence has a strange welding effect and often leads not only to a deeper commitment to

* Marie Noël, *Notes Intimes*, p. 248.
† J. Neville Ward, *The Use of Praying*, p. 127.

God but also to each other. It may seem strange that the solitude that results from silence should have this binding effect, but then, alone with God we begin to discover our true selves. And it is the real self meeting with the real selves of others that leads to true community and that, surely, is a foretaste of what we call heaven.

APPENDIX

Some extracts from the written work of thirteen- to fourteen-year-old girls who followed the course on personal relationships.

What are friends?

A friend is a person, male or female, whom one can trust and take into one's confidence. A person on whom one can depend in times of trouble, sorrow or happiness.

A person may have hundreds of acquaintances but only a few true friends, because should one confide in all his or her friends, the information divulged is no longer a confidence, it becomes public knowledge.

One's childhood friendships are generally superficial. For example: little Mary Brown makes friends with Sarah-Jane, because Sarah-Jane has been given a doll's pram for a Christmas present and Mary wishes to play with it. John hurriedly makes friends with Fred who lives over the road because Fred has two toffee apples and John hopes that Fred will give him one of them.

As one grows older one is drawn to one's friends for the quality of personality rather than the quality of their possessions.

Man is a social creature. He needs people, friends. Whilst the joys of a desert island may appeal to him for a while, after a few weeks he would sadly miss human company, friends. His thoughts would begin to turn to escape.

As a child grows up and becomes an adolescent he requires privacy and a chance to work things out for himself, by trial and error. In some matters, parents are the last people he wishes to confide in or to consult. It is therefore the role of a friend to listen and advise.

One's best friend cannot necessarily give the best advice, concerning various problems, but tension can often be released by talking. Every teenager has someone to whom he or she can talk. An adolescent often likes to be in solitude (self-enforced). Solitude is chosen, whereas being alone is not. One can often feel more lonely when one is with a crowd than when one is not with anyone, alone.

A true friendship can never be broken up without regret. Often school-girl or boy friendships are carried on into married life, by letters or visits. Friends are friends partly by nature of being there in times of trouble. They take your side. If a problem occurs within a family, friends cannot really be of much assistance. In times of financial trouble they come to your aid!

A friend may not necessarily be of the same age-group, but a friend is a friend.

Relationships with parents

Some parents have no doubts at all, about always being right. They try to domineer over their children, and sometimes, unfortunately, succeed. By various tactics they prevent their sons and daughters from doing what they quite reasonably want to do. They stop them from becoming people in their own right, or seriously hamper and slow down the process. Sometimes the tactics are straightforward browbeating and intimidation. For example: one very powerful and dogmatic father threatened to end his very gifted son's career if he did not get his hair cut short. It is necessary that parents have a certain amount of control over their teenage sons and daughters but not to the extent of allowing them so little freedom that they become tense and unhappy. On the other hand parents must not exert too little authority, and so allow too much freedom, thus causing their son or daughter to feel insecure and unhappy.

THE NEED FOR SOLITUDE

There is a great deal of difference between solitude and loneliness. Solitude is chosen and parents must realise that their children want to be alone sometimes. Children must also respect their brothers' and sisters' wishes if they want to be alone too. Friendlessness is really another word for loneliness which is not a choice but forced upon one.

THE NEED FOR TRUST

Trust is most important, the parents need to trust the child to a certain extent and the child must trust the parent. When parents say that you must be home at a certain time, you must trust that it is because they love you. On the other hand, the parents must not make the time too early, they must trust that the child is ready to look after himself.

It will be harmful if too much freedom is given all at once. The child does not know what to do with it and becomes confused, insecure and unhappy.

FATHER

Fathers have a reputation for being unsympathetic but this is not so.

Maybe we got this feeling because when we were children it was always mother who fed us, nursed us and played with us while father was out at work and seemed rather a distant figure.

But fathers can be just as understanding as mothers, maybe more so because they see things from a different viewpoint. So go on, give dad a chance.

WHY WON'T WE ADMIT WHEN WE ARE WRONG?

I think that the cause of this trouble is pride. Nobody likes to admit to being wrong but if you have just had a heated argument with someone and then you realise that you were wrong all along, you would not have the courage to say so (unless you were a very strong character) because you would feel a fool. If you go and admit to being wrong you can never tell what the other person is going to do, they might laugh or sneer or if they were decent he or she might say 'That's all right' and then (for me at least) everything would seem all right, but you would still feel rather foolish deep down.

WHAT IN DAILY LIFE DO PARENTS CRITICIZE MOST?

Some parents do not like their children to speak badly and complain when their children use slang or swear words.

This is probably because they had a stricter upbringing than their children, and were not allowed to use slang. They want to be proud of their children and so when they hear them using bad language they decide to 'nip it in the bud'.

Some parents do not like their children to wear modern clothes and make-up. Modern clothes may seem ugly and queer to parents as in their day, minis and see-thru's were unheard of. They do not want to see their children going around making fools of themselves. (At least that's what they think!) To a parent eye make-up and lip gloss, etc., seem ugly, unnecessary and a waste of money. This is really the generation gap coming in, as they cannot understand why their children want it.

Appearance

Looking in mirrors is natural and necessary (to see whether you need to tidy up or not) unless it is overdone. The right amount of time must be spent in front of your mirror—not so little that you could not care less about your appearance—not so much that you are in love with your face, or despairing of your ugliness as both have bad results.

Beauty is the personality of someone shining through their face. Often when you look at a 'beautiful' girl her features have taken apart may be very ordinary but it is her whole face that is vivacious and alive—sparkling with personality.

Personality makes one beautiful but EVERYONE can be attractive, just by using what they've been given.

With healthy hair in a style that suits you, a clean look and just the right amount of make-up and a big smile you could look fantastic.

What do we mean by love?

To answer that question one must ask what we do not mean by love? We do not mean infatuation, physical attraction or lust.

In the Bible, 1 Corinthians 13 tells of Christian love. This is more than simply the love a husband has for his wife.

Love is a human emotion, it wants to give rather than to receive, to honour not degrade; true love leads to the desire for the fusion of two persons (not just physically).

In a young couple, the fellow thinks more of his girl friend than of himself, and she is willing to put herself out to please him. Love is selfless.

LOVE IS . . .

Love is respect or reverence for another person and wanting only their highest good.

This definition of love can apply to all people, the opposite sex, parents, friends, fellow workers and brothers and sisters.

Love is total giving of oneself to the other. Love expresses itself by giving, it wants to give the very best and does not count the cost.

AN ENGAGEMENT RING

An engagement ring is now considered as a traditional symbol and is not essential. It may not be practical to have a ring if the boy is still a student or cannot afford it, and it may cause a lot of anxiety to the girl if it is expensive and she is not used to wearing a ring. What you pay for it is not important, the thought behind it is. When an engagement ring is worn, it is an open mark of commitment.

Part of the preparation for marriage during the engagement period is planning the future home. The course included advice on how to get a mortgage and buy a house.

A BUILDING SOCIETY

A building society is a firm that lends money for purchasing property. If you wanted to buy a house, you would not be able to save enough money for it, so you would go to a building society to borrow some.

Before you can have the money, the building society has to know if the house is worth what you are going to pay for it, so you hire a surveyor to look it over for you. If the house is in good condition you then have to fill in forms about your income, how many children you have, and so on, to make sure that you are able to pay back the money and interest.

Depending on the condition of the house and your income, you could get a mortgage for up to ninety per cent of the value of the house. You would not, however, be able to get one for the whole value, because if you cannot repay the money, the building society will sell the house to get its money back. If it lends you all the money, there is no margin for deterioration in the value.

The building society gets its money from investment: people invest their money for an interest, and the building society lends that money to other people as mortgages for a greater interest.

LOVE MUST GIVE

Clyde so loved Bonnie that he gave her an expensive diamond ring.

The girl so loved her kitten that she gave up her pocket money to buy it some fish.

The boy so loved his friend that he gave up his free time to find his homework.

My parents so loved me that they gave me an expensive holiday.

God so loved the world that he gave his only begotten Son, that whosoever believeth in him should not perish, but have everlasting life.

SEX BEFORE MARRIAGE

(An imaginary discussion between a young couple, written by a thirteen-year-old girl.)

MARY: Supposing I get pregnant, we would have to start our married life as a ready made family.

JOHN: Oh there's no risk these days with modern contraceptives.

MARY: But John, things can go wrong, after all no contraceptive is foolproof. Not one is a hundred per cent safe.

JOHN: Yes, but darling we can be extra careful, I feel sure that it will be all right.

MARY: Mmmm. Once we've done it things will never be the same again.

JOHN: It can only bring us closer together.

MARY: John you must know that a woman needs a sense of utter security and a permanent relationship. . . .

JOHN: Well, we're engaged —

MARY: Let me finish. A woman has to be completely secure and free from all fears and tensions, surrounded by love to enjoy it. I think that I'd feel afraid.

JOHN: What of?

MARY: Pregnancy, being found out—why we might find that we weren't suited.

JOHN: Better to find out now than when we're married.

MARY: No, that's different! When you're married you've got time, you're secure, there's time to adapt.

JOHN: All right darling, I can see that you wouldn't be happy. We'll wait till our honeymoon then and carry on as we are.

MARY: Thank you, darling.

Girls were also encouraged to include imaginative illustrations in their project folder. Here are two examples.

The first was a quotation from *'Facing Life's Challenge'* by J. Hills-Cotterill.

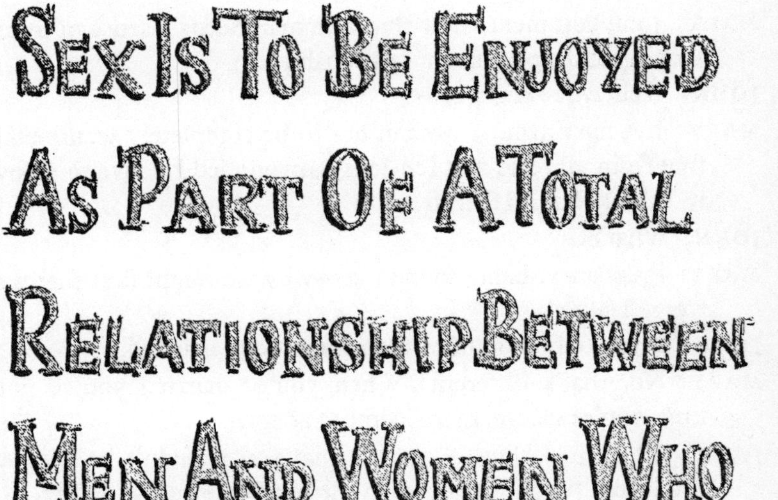

The Right Blend

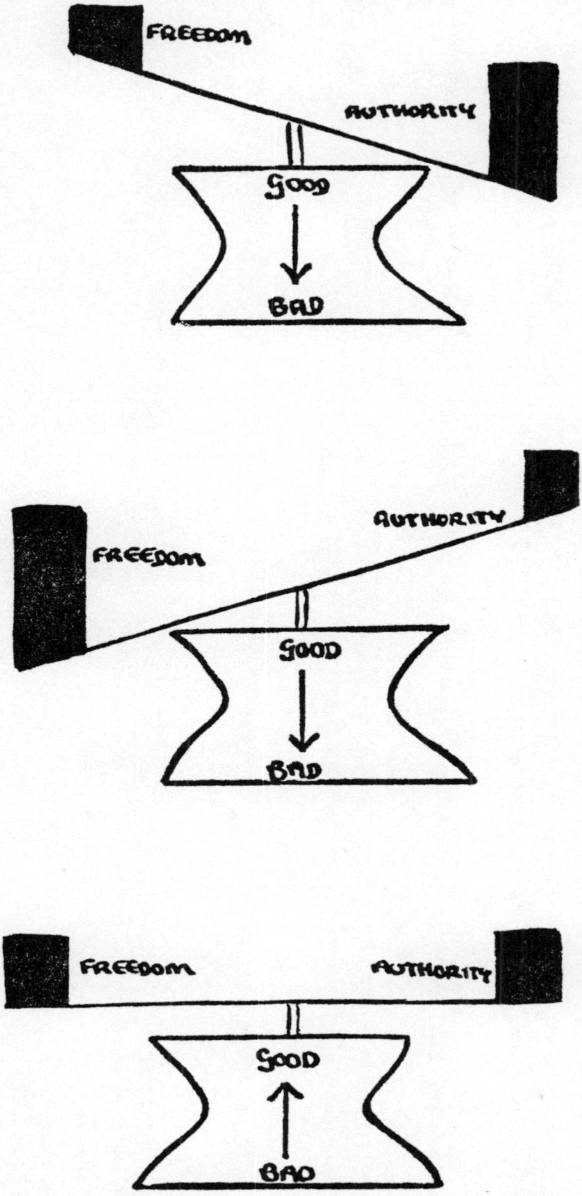

FOR FURTHER REFERENCE

BIBLE BACKGROUND

The Way it was in Bible Times, Merrill T. Gilbertson (Lutterworth)
The World in which Jesus Lived, Basil Mathews (O.U.P.)
In the Steps of Jesus, H. V. Morton (Methuen)
Jesus of Nazareth, Joy Harrington (Brockhampton Press)
The Palestine of Jesus, Bernard Youngman (Hulton Ed. Pubns.)
Dictionary of Life in Bible Times, W. Corswant (Hodder & Stoughton)
Bible Encyclopaedia for Children, Cecil Northcott (Lutterworth)
Susan in the Land of the Bible, Sven and Pia Gillsater (Heinemann)
Bible Background, J. W. D. Smith (Methuen)
The Bible Guidebook, M. Entwistle (S.C.M.)
The World Christ Knew, A. C. Deane (Eyre & Spottiswoode)
The Living World of the New Testament, H. C. Kee and F. W. Young (Darton, Longman & Todd)

ATLASES

Atlas of the Bible, L. H. Grollenberg (Nelson)
Westminster Smaller Atlas (S.C.M.)
Wall Atlas of Bible Lands (series of 8) (G. Philip)
Behold the Land (a pictorial atlas of the Bible), F. H. Hilliard (G. Philip)

ARCHAEOLOGY

Illustrations from Biblical Archaeology, D. J. Wiseman (Tyndale)
Biblical Archaeology, G. E. Wright (Duckworth)
Light from the Ancient Past, J. Finegan (O.U.P.)

The Bible as History, W. Keller (Hodder & Stoughton)
The Bible as History in Pictures, W. Keller (Hodder & Stoughton)

ETHICS

An Exposition of Christian Sex Ethics, V. A. Demant (Hodder & Stoughton)
Honest to God, J. A. T. Robinson (S.C.M.)
God, Sex and War, D. M. Mackinnon (Fontana)
The Four Loves, C. S. Lewis (Fontana)
Remarriage and Mixed Marriage, H. Montefiore (S.P.C.K.)

COMPARATIVE RELIGIONS

The Religions of Mankind, H. K. Luce (Chatto Educ.)
Concise Encyclopaedia of Living Faiths, R. C. Zaehner (Hutchinson)
World Religions: a dialogue, N. Smart (Penguin)
The Religions of the World, G. E. Phillips (R.E.P.)
How Men Worship, F. H. Hilliard (Routledge & Kegan Paul)
Men Seeking God, C. Mayhew (Allen & Unwin)
A Short Comparative History of Religions, T. H. Robinson (Duckworth)

PRACTICAL CLASSROOM WORK

The Art of Mime, I. Mawer (Methuen)
Choral Speaking, M. Gullan (Methuen)
Religion through Drama, M. Sims Williams (S.C.M.)
Project Work in Religious Education, R. L. Arundale (R.E.P.)
Models for the Scripture Lesson, M. Barwell (N.S.S.U.)
Making Bible Models, H. W. Whanslaw (R.E.P.)
More Bible Models and How to Make Them, H. W. Whanslaw (R.E.P.)
Marionettes and Rod Puppets, H. W. Whanslaw (R.E.P.)
Model Ways to Bible Lands, Minnie Clark (Victory Press)
Themes in Religious Education for Nines to Thirteens, K. N. Smith (Macmillan)
Discuss and Discover, Charles Martin (S.U.)
Let's Discuss, J. Hills-Cotterill (S.U.)

To Do and To Know, Jennifer Ferguson (R.E.P.)

Living Light, *Growing Christian*, *Schools' Study Bible*, *Living Bible*, (R.E.P. Project)

Project Work for Juniors (Homes, Neighbours, Senses) D. J. Taylor (Lutterworth)

GENERAL

Religious Thinking and Religious Education, K. Howkins (Tyndale)

Changing Aims in Religious Education, E. Cox (Routledge & Kegan Paul)

Readiness for Religion, R. Goldman (Routledge & Kegan Paul)

We Teach Them Wrong, R. Acland (Gollancz)

New Ground in Christian Education, H. Loukes (S.C.M.)

Tennage Religion, H. Loukes (S.C.M.)

The New Religious Education, H. F. Mathews (Chester House Publications)

Revolution in Religious Education, H. F. Mathews (R.E.P.)

Children in Search of Meaning, Violet Made (S.C.M.)

The Moral Judgment of the Child, J. Piaget (Routledge & Kegan Paul)

INDEX